The Ultimate Crock Pot
Cookbook for Beginners

1800 Days of Creative, Tasty and Easy Recipes for Every Slow Cooking Meal and Occasion, from Breakfast to Desserts, Snacks, Lunch and Dinner

Milton E. Armstrong

Table of Contents

Chapter 8 Desserts   58

Chapter 10 Pizzas, Wraps, and Sandwiches 79

Appendix Measurement Conversion Chart 81

INTRODUCTION

Hi there! I'm the author of The Ultimate Crock Pot Cookbook for Beginners, and I'm so excited to share my love of slow-cooking with you! If you're tired of slaving over a hot stove or just looking for an easy way to make delicious, home-cooked meals, then this cookbook is for you.

The Ultimate Crock Pot Cookbook for Beginners is a comprehensive guide to cooking delicious and healthy meals with the convenience of a slow cooker. This book is different because it's specifically designed for beginners who want to learn how to use a crock pot effectively. It features easy-to-follow recipes that are perfect for busy people who want to save time and effort in the kitchen. The book covers a wide range of cuisines, from Italian to Asian, and includes recipes for soups, stews, and even desserts! With this book, you'll be able to create mouth-watering meals that are both healthy and flavorful.

If you ask me, "why crock pot?" Then I would tell you that crock pot cooking is an excellent way to prepare healthy meals, especially for people with busy schedules. It is a convenient and easy way to cook meals while you attend to other tasks. Crock pot cooking is also beneficial for individuals who want to reduce their intake of processed foods since it encourages the use of fresh, whole ingredients. Additionally, crock pot cooking is a cost-effective way to prepare meals since it uses less energy than conventional oven cooking. Overall, using a crock pot can help make meal preparation easier, healthier, and more affordable.

With over 100 mouth-watering recipes that are simple to prepare and packed with flavor, you'll be a crock pot pro in no time. So grab your slow cooker and let's get cooking!

Chapter 1 Breakfasts

Strawberries and Cream Overnight Oatmeal

Prep time: 5 minutes | Cook time: 4 to 5 hours |

Serves 4 to 6

Nonstick cooking spray (optional)

1¼ cups steel-cut oats

4 cups water

1⅔ cups unsweetened plant-based milk

2 teaspoons vanilla extract

¼ cup maple syrup (optional)

3 tablespoons ground flaxseed

1 pound (454 g) fresh strawberries, stemmed and sliced

1. Coat the inside of the crock pot with cooking spray (if using) or line it with a crock pot liner. 2. Place the oats, water, milk, vanilla, and maple syrup (if using) in the crock pot. Cover and cook on High for 4 to 5 hours or on Low for 8 to 9 hours. 3. When ready to serve, stir the flaxseed into the oatmeal and portion into bowls. Top each with 3 to 5 sliced strawberries.

Sweet Potato and Black Bean Hash

Prep time: 10 minutes | Cook time: 2 to 3 hours |

Serves 4 to 6

1 shallot, diced

2 cups peeled, chopped sweet potatoes (about 1 large or 2 small)

1 medium bell pepper (any color), diced

2 garlic cloves, minced

1 (14½-ounce / 411-g) can

black beans, drained and rinsed

1 teaspoon paprika

½ teaspoon onion powder

½ teaspoon garlic powder

¼ cup store-bought low-sodium vegetable broth

4 to 6 tablespoons unsweetened plant-based milk

1. Place the shallot, sweet potatoes, bell pepper, garlic, beans, paprika, onion powder, garlic powder, and broth in the crock pot. Stir to combine. Cover and cook on Low for 2 to 3 hours, until the potatoes are soft. 2. Remove the lid and add the milk, starting with 4 tablespoons, and stir to combine. You're looking for a creamy sauce to develop. Add more milk as needed and allow to heat through for a few minutes before serving.

Golden Beet and Spinach Frittata

Prep time: 15 minutes | Cook time: 5 to 7 hours |

Serves 4 to 6

1 tablespoon extra-virgin olive oil

8 large eggs

1 cup packed fresh spinach leaves, chopped

1 cup diced peeled golden beets

½ medium onion, diced

¼ cup unsweetened almond milk

¾ teaspoon sea salt

½ teaspoon garlic powder

½ teaspoon dried basil leaves

Freshly ground black pepper, to taste

1. Coat the crock pot with the olive oil. 2. In a large bowl, combine the eggs, spinach, beets, onion, almond milk, salt, garlic powder, and basil, and season with pepper. Whisk together and pour the custard into the crock pot. 3. Cover the cooker and set to low. Cook for 5 to 7 hours, or until the eggs are completely set, and serve.

Three-Grain Granola

Prep time: 15 minutes | Cook time: 5 hours | Serves 40

5 cups regular oatmeal

4 cups barley flakes

3 cups buckwheat flakes

2 cups whole almonds

2 cups whole walnuts

½ cup honey

2 teaspoons ground cinnamon

1 tablespoon vanilla extract

2 cups golden raisins

2 cups dried cherries

1. In a 6-quart crock pot, mix the oatmeal, barley flakes, buckwheat flakes, almonds, and walnuts. 2. In a small bowl, mix the honey, cinnamon, and vanilla, and mix well. Drizzle this mixture over the food in the crock pot and stir with a spatula to coat. 3. Partially cover the crock pot. Cook on low for 3½ to 5 hours, stirring twice during cooking time, until the oatmeal, barley and buckwheat flakes, and nuts are toasted. 4. Remove the granola from the crock pot and spread on two large baking sheets. Add the raisins and cherries to the granola and stir gently. 5. Let the granola cool, then store in an airtight container at room temperature.

Streusel Cake

Prep time: 10 minutes | Cook time: 3 to 4 hours | Serves 8 to 10

1 (16-ounce / 454-g) package pound cake mix, prepared according to package directions
¼ cup packed brown sugar
1 tablespoon flour
¼ cup chopped nuts
1 teaspoon cinnamon

1. Liberally grease and flour a 2-pound (907-g) coffee can, or crock pot baking insert, that fits into your crock pot. Pour prepared cake mix into coffee can or baking insert. 2. In a small bowl, mix brown sugar, flour, nuts, and cinnamon together. Sprinkle over top of cake mix. 3. Place coffee tin or baking insert in crock pot. Cover top of tin or insert with several layers of paper towels. 4. Cover cooker itself and cook on high 3 to 4 hours, or until toothpick inserted in center of cake comes out clean. 5. Remove baking tin from crock pot and allow to cool for 30 minutes before cutting into wedges to serve.

Egg White Vegetable Frittata

Prep time: 10 minutes | Cook time: 6 to 8 hours | Serves 8 to 12

Nonstick cooking spray
2 cups egg whites (from about 12 large eggs)
1½ cups chopped vegetables (spinach, tomatoes, bell peppers, mushrooms, etc.)
½ cup grated low-fat Cheddar
cheese
½ cup low-fat or skim milk
1 garlic clove, minced
¼ cup diced onion
Salt, to taste
Freshly ground black pepper, to taste

1. Spray the crock pot generously with nonstick cooking spray. 2. In a large bowl, whisk together the egg whites, vegetables, cheese, milk, garlic, and onion. Season lightly with salt and pepper, and pour into the crock pot. 3. Cook on low for 6 to 8 hours, or until the eggs are set, and serve.

Hot Wheat Berry Cereal

Prep time: 5 minutes | Cook time: 10 hours | Serves 4

1 cup wheat berries
5 cups water

1. Rinse and sort berries. Cover with water and soak all day (or 8 hours) in crock pot. 2. Cover. Cook on low overnight (or 10 hours). 3. Drain, if needed. Serve.

Egg and Wild Rice Casserole

Prep time: 20 minutes | Cook time: 7 hours | Serves 6

3 cups plain cooked wild rice
2 cups sliced mushrooms
1 red bell pepper, stemmed, seeded, and chopped
1 onion, minced
2 garlic cloves, minced
11 eggs
1 teaspoon dried thyme leaves
¼ teaspoon salt
1½ cups shredded Swiss cheese

1. In a 6-quart crock pot, layer the wild rice, mushrooms, bell pepper, onion, and garlic. 2. In a large bowl, beat the eggs with the thyme and salt. Pour into the crock pot. Top with the cheese. 3. Cover and cook on low for 5 to 7 hours, or until a food thermometer registers 165ºF (74ºC) and the casserole is set.

Banana Bread Oatmeal

Prep time: 20 minutes | Cook time: 8 hours | Serves 8

4 cups coconut milk
4 cups water
2 cups steel cut oats
3 ripe bananas, peeled and mashed
⅓ cup coconut sugar
2 teaspoons ground cinnamon
½ teaspoon ground nutmeg
2 teaspoons vanilla extract
1 cup chopped pecans

1. Combine the coconut milk and water in a 6-quart crock pot. Add the steel cut oats, bananas, coconut sugar, cinnamon, nutmeg, vanilla, and pecans. 2. Cover and cook on low for 7 to 8 hours or until the oats are very tender. Stir well before serving.

Breakfast Sausage

Prep time: 5 minutes | Cook time: 6 to 8 hours | Serves 8

1 pound (454 g) lean ground pork
1 garlic clove, minced
1 teaspoon salt
1 teaspoon dried thyme
½ teaspoon dried oregano
½ teaspoon onion powder
¼ teaspoon freshly ground black pepper
¼ teaspoon paprika
¼ teaspoon ground cinnamon

1. In a large mixing bowl, combine the pork, garlic, salt, thyme, oregano, onion powder, pepper, paprika, and cinnamon. 2. Press the meat mixture evenly into the bottom of the crock pot. 3. Cook on low for 6 to 8 hours, or until the meat is completely cooked through. 4. Blot any extra grease off the top, if needed, using a paper towel. 5. Transfer the meat to a cutting board, cut the sausage into squares or circles, and serve.

Easy Egg and Sausage Puff

Prep time: 15 minutes | Cook time: 2 to 2½ hours | Serves 6

1 pound (454 g) loose sausage
6 eggs
1 cup all-purpose baking mix
1 cup shredded Cheddar cheese
2 cups milk
¼ teaspoon dry mustard (optional)
Nonstick cooking spray

1. Brown sausage in nonstick skillet. Break up chunks of meat as it cooks. Drain. 2. Meanwhile, spray interior of crock pot with nonstick cooking spray. 3. Mix all ingredients in crock pot. 4. Cover and cook on high 1 hour. Turn to low and cook 1 to 1½ hours, or until the dish is fully cooked in the center.

"Baked" Oatmeal

Prep time: 10 minutes | Cook time: 2½ to 3 hours | Serves 4 to 6

⅓ cup oil
½ cup sugar
1 large egg, beaten
2 cups dry quick oats
1½ teaspoons baking powder
½ teaspoon salt
¾ cup milk

1. Pour the oil into the crock pot to grease bottom and sides. 2. Add remaining ingredients. Mix well. 3. Cook on low 2½ to 3 hours.

Welsh Rarebit

Prep time: 10 minutes | Cook time: 1½ to 2½ hours | Serves 6 to 8

1 (12-ounce / 340-g) can beer
1 tablespoon dry mustard
1 teaspoon Worcestershire sauce
½ teaspoon salt
⅛ teaspoon black or white pepper
1 pound (454 g) American
cheese, cubed
1 pound (454 g) sharp Cheddar cheese, cubed
English muffins or toast
Tomato slices
Bacon, cooked until crisp
Fresh steamed asparagus spears

1. In crock pot, combine beer, mustard, 2. Worcestershire sauce, salt, and pepper. Cover and cook on high 1 to 2 hours, until mixture boils. 3. Add cheese, a little at a time, stirring constantly until all the cheese melts. 4. Heat on high 20 to 30 minutes with cover off, stirring frequently. 5. Serve hot over toasted English muffins or over toasted bread cut into triangles. Garnish with tomato slices, strips of crisp bacon and steamed asparagus spears.

Dulce Leche

Prep time: 5 minutes | Cook time: 2 hours | Makes 2½ cups

2 (14-ounce / 397-g) cans sweetened condensed milk
Cookies, for serving

1. Place unopened cans of milk in crock pot. Fill cooker with warm water so that it comes above the cans by 1½ to 2 inches. 2. Cover cooker. Cook on high 2 hours. 3. Cool unopened cans. 4. When opened, the contents should be thick and spreadable. Use as a filling between 2 cookies.

Breakfast Fruit Compote

Prep time: 5 minutes | Cook time: 2 to 7 hours | Serves 8 to 9

1 (12-ounce / 340-g) package dried apricots
1 (12-ounce / 340-g) package pitted dried plums
1 (11-ounce / 312-g) can mandarin oranges in light
syrup, undrained
1 (29-ounce / 822-g) can sliced peaches in light syrup, undrained
¼ cup white raisins
10 maraschino cherries

1.Combine all ingredients in crock pot. Mix well. 2. Cover. Cook on low 6 to 7 hours, or on high 2 to 3 hours.

Overnight Apple Oatmeal

Prep time: 10 minutes | Cook time: 6 to 8 hours | Serves 4

2 cups skim or 2% milk
2 tablespoons honey, or ¼ cup brown sugar
1 tablespoon margarine
¼ teaspoon salt
½ teaspoon ground cinnamon
1 cup dry rolled oats
1 cup apples, chopped
½ cup raisins (optional)
¼ cup walnuts, chopped
½ cup fat-free half-and-half

1. Spray inside of crock pot with nonfat cooking spray. 2. In a mixing bowl, combine all ingredients except half-and-half. Pour into cooker. 3. Cover and cook on low overnight, ideally 6 to 8 hours. The oatmeal is ready to eat in the morning. 4. Stir in the half-and-half just before serving.

Breakfast Hominy

Prep time: 5 minutes | Cook time: 8 hours | Serves 5

1 cup dry cracked hominy
1 teaspoon salt
Black pepper (optional)

3 cups water
2 tablespoons butter

1. Stir all ingredients together in a greased crock pot. 2. Cover and cook on low 8 hours, or overnight. 3. Serve warm for breakfast.

crock pot Oatmeal

Prep time: 15 minutes | Cook time: 8 to 9 hours | Serves 7 to 8

2 cups dry rolled oats
4 cups water
1 large apple, peeled and chopped

1 cup raisins
1 teaspoon cinnamon
1 to 2 tablespoons orange zest

1. Combine all ingredients in your crock pot. 2. Cover and cook on low 8 to 9 hours. 3. Serve topped with brown sugar, if you wish, and milk.

Nutty Granola with Power Seeds and Dried Fruit

Prep time: 15 minutes | Cook time: 6 hours | Makes 10 cups

1 overripe banana, peeled
3 tablespoons water
6 cups old-fashioned oats
½ cup chopped pecans
½ cup chopped walnuts
½ cup raw cashews
½ cup slivered or chopped raw almonds
½ cup unsweetened coconut flakes
3 tablespoons ground flaxseed

3 tablespoons raw pepitas
3 tablespoons raw sunflower seeds
3 tablespoons chia seeds
½ cup maple syrup (optional)
½ cup aquafaba
½ cup raisins
½ cup currants
½ cup unsweetened dried cherries

1. In the bottom of the crock pot, mash together the banana and water. Add the oats, pecans, walnuts, cashews, almonds, coconut, flaxseed, pepitas, sunflower seeds, chia seeds, and maple syrup (if using). 2. In a small bowl, use an electric beater to whip the aquafaba into almost-stiff peaks, about 5 minutes. Add it to the crock pot and stir to combine. 3. To keep the condensation that forms on the inside of the lid away from the granola, stretch a clean dish towel or several layers of paper towels over the top of the crock pot, but not touching the food, and place the lid on top of the towel(s). Cook on Low for 6 hours, stirring every hour to make sure the granola does not burn and replacing the damp towels as needed. 4. After 6 hours, the granola will be darker in color. Transfer it to a parchment-lined baking sheet, spread it out, and let it cool for up to 1 hour. Once it's completely cool and crispy, sprinkle on the raisins, currants, and dried cherries and stir to combine. Store in a large airtight container for up to 2 weeks.

Sweet Potato Home Fries

Prep time: 15 minutes | Cook time: 6 to 8 hours | Serves 4 to 6

3 tablespoons extra-virgin olive oil, plus more for coating the crock pot
2 pounds (907 g) sweet potatoes, diced
1 red bell pepper, seeded and diced

½ medium onion, finely diced
1 teaspoon garlic powder
1 teaspoon sea salt
1 teaspoon dried rosemary, minced
½ teaspoon freshly ground black pepper

1. Coat the crock pot with a thin layer of olive oil. 2. Put the sweet potatoes in the crock pot, along with the red bell pepper and onion. Drizzle the olive oil as evenly as possible over the vegetables. 3. Sprinkle in the garlic powder, salt, rosemary, and pepper. Toss evenly to coat the sweet potatoes in the oil and seasonings. 4. Cover the cooker and set to low. Cook for 6 to 8 hours and serve.

Savory Basil Oatmeal

Prep time: 10 minutes | Cook time: 8 hours | Serves 8

3 cups steel-cut oatmeal
2 shallots, peeled and minced
5 cups vegetable broth
1 cup water
1 teaspoon dried basil leaves
½ teaspoon dried thyme leaves
¼ teaspoon salt

¼ teaspoon freshly ground black pepper
½ cup grated Parmesan cheese
2 cups chopped baby spinach leaves
2 tablespoons chopped fresh basil

1. In a 6-quart crock pot, mix the oatmeal, shallots, vegetable broth, water, basil, thyme, salt, and pepper. Cover and cook on low for 7 to 8 hours, or until the oatmeal is tender. 2. Stir in the Parmesan cheese, spinach, and basil, and let stand, covered, for another 5 minutes. Stir and serve.

Cranberry-Quinoa Hot Cereal

Prep time: 15 minutes | Cook time: 8 hours | Serves 12

3 cups quinoa, rinsed and drained	¼ cup honey
2 cups unsweetened apple juice	1 teaspoon vanilla extract
4 cups canned coconut milk	1 teaspoon ground cinnamon
2 cups water	½ teaspoon salt
	1½ cups dried cranberries

1. In a 6-quart crock pot, mix all of the ingredients. Cover and cook on low for 6 to 8 hours or until the quinoa is creamy.

Root Vegetable Hash

Prep time: 20 minutes | Cook time: 8 hours | Serves 8

4 Yukon Gold potatoes, chopped	2 onions, chopped
2 russet potatoes, chopped	2 garlic cloves, minced
1 large parsnip, peeled and chopped	2 tablespoons olive oil
3 large carrots, peeled and chopped	¼ cup vegetable broth
	½ teaspoon salt
	1 teaspoon dried thyme leaves

1. In a 6-quart crock pot, mix all of the ingredients. Cover and cook on low for 7 to 8 hours. 2. Stir the hash well and serve.

Carrot and Fennel Quinoa Breakfast Casserole

Prep time: 15 minutes | Cook time: 5 to 7 hours | Serves 4 to 6

6 large eggs	Freshly ground black pepper, to taste
½ cup quinoa, rinsed well	
1½ cups unsweetened almond milk	1 fennel bulb, finely sliced
½ teaspoon sea salt	3 medium carrots, diced
½ teaspoon garlic powder	1 tablespoon extra-virgin olive oil
¼ teaspoon dried oregano	

1. In a medium bowl, whisk the eggs. 2. Add the quinoa, almond milk, salt, garlic powder, and oregano, and season with pepper. Whisk well until all ingredients are combined. 3. Stir in the fennel and carrots. 4. Coat the crock pot with the olive oil, and slowly pour in the egg mixture. 5. Cover the cooker and set to low. Cook for 5 to 7 hours and serve.

Southwestern-Style Breakfast Burritos

Prep time: 10 minutes | Cook time: 2 to 3 hours | Serves 4 to 6

1 medium onion, diced	2 heaping cups)
1 medium red bell pepper, diced	1 (14-ounce / 397-g) package extra-firm tofu
3 garlic cloves, minced	1 teaspoon ground turmeric
1 (10-ounce / 283-g) package frozen corn	1 tablespoon chili powder
1 (14-ounce / 397-g) can pinto beans, drained and rinsed	3 tablespoons nutritional yeast
1 (14-ounce / 397-g) can no-salt-added diced tomatoes	Salt (optional)
2 handfuls chopped kale (about	Ground black pepper
	6 to 8 (10-inch) whole-grain tortillas

1. Place the onion, bell pepper, and garlic in the crock pot. Add the corn, beans, tomatoes, and kale. Crumble the tofu over the vegetables to look like scrambled eggs. Sprinkle the turmeric over the tofu and stir to coat, until the tofu is the color of scrambled eggs. Add the chili powder, nutritional yeast, salt (if using), and black pepper. Stir to combine. Cover and cook on High for 2 to 3 hours or on Low for 5 to 6 hours. 2. Using a slotted spoon to drain off excess liquid, scoop about ⅓ cup of burrito filling onto the center of each tortilla. Roll the bottom of the tortilla to cover the filling, fold one side over the filling, and continue rolling to close.

Baked Berry Oatmeal

Prep time: 15 minutes | Cook time: 6 hours | Serves 12

7 cups rolled oats	¼ teaspoon salt
4 eggs	1 teaspoon ground cinnamon
1½ cups almond milk	¼ teaspoon ground ginger
2 tablespoons melted coconut oil	1½ cups dried blueberries
⅓ cup honey	1 cup dried cherries

1. Grease a 6-quart crock pot with plain vegetable oil. 2. In a large bowl, place the rolled oats. 3. In a medium bowl, mix the eggs, almond milk, coconut oil, honey, salt, cinnamon, and ginger. Mix until well combined. Pour this mixture over the oats. 4. Gently stir in the dried blueberries and dried cherries. Pour into the prepared crock pot. 5. Cover and cook on low for 4 to 6 hours, or until the oatmeal mixture is set and the edges start to brown.

Eggs in Purgatory

Prep time: 15 minutes | Cook time: 8 hours | Serves 8

2½ pounds (1.1 kg) Roma tomatoes, chopped	½ teaspoon dried marjoram leaves
2 onions, chopped	1 cup vegetable broth
2 garlic cloves, chopped	8 large eggs
1 teaspoon paprika	2 red chili peppers, minced
½ teaspoon ground cumin	½ cup chopped flat-leaf parsley

1. In a 6-quart crock pot, mix the tomatoes, onions, garlic, paprika, cumin, marjoram, and vegetable broth, and stir to mix. Cover and cook on low for 7 to 8 hours, or until a sauce has formed. 2. One at a time, break the eggs into the sauce; do not stir. 3. Cover and cook on high until the egg whites are completely set and the yolk is thickened, about 20 minutes. Sprinkle the eggs with the minced red chili peppers. 4. Sprinkle with the parsley and serve.

Simple Steel-Cut Oats

Prep time: 15 minutes | Cook time: 6 to 8 hours |
Serves 4 to 6

1 tablespoon coconut oil	½ teaspoon sea salt
4 cups boiling water	1 cup steel-cut oats

1. Coat the crock pot with the coconut oil. 2. In your crock pot, combine the boiling water, salt, and oats. 3. Cover the cooker and set to warm (or low if there is no warm setting). Cook for 6 to 8 hours and serve.

Blueberry, Cinnamon, and Pecan French Toast
Prep time: 10 minutes | Cook time: 2 to 3 hours | Serves 4 to 6

2 tablespoons ground flaxseed	1 teaspoon ground cinnamon
5 tablespoons water	1 tablespoon vanilla extract
1 (16-ounce / 454-g) loaf crusty whole-grain bread	Nonstick cooking spray (optional)
1 overripe banana, peeled	2 cups fresh or frozen blueberries, divided
1 (14½-ounce / 411-g) can full-fat coconut milk	¼ cup chopped pecans, for serving
1 cup unsweetened plant-based milk	Maple syrup, for serving (optional)
1 tablespoon chia seeds	

1. In a small bowl or ramekin, stir together the flaxseed and water to form flax eggs. Let rest while preparing the remaining ingredients. 2. Slice the bread into 1- to 2-inch chunks and place in a large casserole dish deep enough to have the bread submerged in the custard. 3. Place the banana, coconut milk, plant-based milk, chia seeds, cinnamon, vanilla, and flax eggs in a blender. Blend to combine and pour over the bread. Cover and refrigerate for at least 30 minutes to allow the bread to soak up the custard. 4. Coat the inside of the crock pot with cooking spray (if using) or line it with a crock pot liner. Remove the bread and custard mixture from refrigerator and place half in the bottom of the crock pot. Add 1 cup of blueberries, then layer the remaining half of the bread and custard mixture. Top with the remaining 1 cup of blueberries. Cover and cook on High for 2 to 3 hours or on Low for 4 to 5 hours. 5. To serve, top each portion with a tablespoon of pecans and a drizzle of maple syrup (if using).

Mediterranean Strata

Prep time: 20 minutes | Cook time: 7 hours | Serves 10

8 cups whole-wheat bread, cut into cubes	leaves
	4 eggs
1 onion, finely chopped	2 egg whites
3 garlic cloves, minced	2 tablespoons olive oil
2 red bell peppers, stemmed, seeded, and chopped	1½ cups 2% milk
	1 cup shredded Asiago cheese
2 cups chopped baby spinach	

1. In a 6-quart crock pot, mix the bread cubes, onion, garlic, bell peppers, and spinach. 2. In a medium bowl, mix the eggs, egg whites, olive oil, and milk, and beat well. Pour this mixture into the crock pot. Sprinkle with the cheese. 3. Cover and cook on low for 5 to 7 hours, or until a food thermometer registers 165°F (74°C) and the strata is set and puffed. 4. Scoop the strata out of the crock pot to serve.

French Vegetable Omelet

Prep time: 20 minutes | Cook time: 4 hours | Serves 6

12 eggs, beaten	1 yellow bell pepper, stemmed, seeded, and chopped
⅓ cup 2% milk	
½ teaspoon dried thyme leaves	1 small zucchini, peeled and diced
½ teaspoon dried tarragon leaves	
	2 shallots, peeled and minced
¼ teaspoon salt	½ cup grated Parmesan cheese
1 cup chopped fresh asparagus	

1. Grease the inside of a 6-quart crock pot with plain vegetable oil. 2. In a large bowl, mix the eggs, milk, thyme, tarragon, and salt, and mix well with an eggbeater or wire whisk until well combined. 3. Add the asparagus, bell pepper, zucchini, and shallots. Pour into the crock pot. 4. Cover and cook on low for 3 to 4 hours, or until the eggs are set. 5. Sprinkle with the Parmesan cheese; cover and cook for another 5 to 10 minutes or until the cheese starts to melt.

Quinoa-Kale-Egg Casserole

Prep time: 20 minutes | Cook time: 8 hours | Serves 8

3 cups 2% milk

1½ cups vegetable broth

11 eggs

1½ cups quinoa, rinsed and drained

3 cups chopped kale

1 leek, chopped

1 red bell pepper, stemmed, seeded, and chopped

3 garlic cloves, minced

1½ cups shredded Havarti cheese

1. Grease a 6-quart crock pot with vegetable oil and set aside. 2. In a large bowl, mix the milk, vegetable broth, and eggs, and beat well with a wire whisk. 3. Stir in the quinoa, kale, leek, bell pepper, garlic, and cheese. Pour this mixture into the prepared crock pot. 4. Cover and cook on low for 6 to 8 hours, or until a food thermometer registers 165°F (74°C) and the mixture is set.

Morning Millet

Prep time: 15 minutes | Cook time: 7 to 8 hours | Serves 4

1 cup millet

2 cups water

2 cups full-fat coconut milk

½ teaspoon sea salt

½ teaspoon ground cinnamon

½ teaspoon ground ginger

¼ teaspoon vanilla extract

½ cup fresh blueberries

1. In your crock pot, combine the millet, water, coconut milk, salt, cinnamon, ginger, and vanilla. Stir well. 2. Cover the cooker and set to low. Cook for 7 to 8 hours. 3. Stir in the blueberries to warm at the end and serve.

Potato and Veggie Breakfast Casserole

Prep time: 10 minutes | Cook time: 4 to 5 hours | Serves 4 to 6

1 medium red bell pepper, diced

1 medium onion, diced

1 (8-ounce / 227-g) package white button or cremini mushrooms, quartered

3 cups chopped kale

Ground black pepper

Salt (optional)

1 teaspoon garlic powder, divided

1 teaspoon onion powder, divided

1 teaspoon paprika, divided

1 (14-ounce / 397-g) package extra-firm tofu, drained

1 teaspoon ground turmeric

8 small Yukon Gold or red potatoes (about 2 pounds / 907 g), unpeeled and sliced into half-inch rounds

1. Place the bell pepper, onion, mushrooms, and kale in the crock pot. Season with pepper and salt (if using). Add ½ teaspoon each of the garlic powder, onion powder, and paprika. Mix to distribute the seasonings. 2. Crumble the tofu directly into the crock pot. Sprinkle the tofu with the turmeric and stir until the tofu is coated. Then mix the tofu and veggies together. 3. Layer the potatoes on top of the veggies and tofu. Sprinkle with the remaining ½ teaspoon each of garlic powder, onion powder, and paprika. Season again with salt (if using) and pepper. Cover and cook on High for 4 to 5 hours or on Low for 7 to 8 hours.

Mixed Berry Honey Granola

Prep time: 15 minutes | Cook time: 5 hours | Makes 20 cups

10 cups rolled oats

2 cups whole almonds

2 cups whole walnuts

2 cups macadamia nuts

½ cup honey

2 teaspoons ground cinnamon

¼ teaspoon ground cardamom

1 tablespoon vanilla extract

2 cups dried blueberries

2 cups dried cherries

1. In a 6-quart crock pot, mix the oatmeal, almonds, walnuts, and macadamia nuts. 2. In a small bowl, mix the honey, cinnamon, cardamom, and vanilla. Drizzle this mixture over the oatmeal mixture in the crock pot and stir with a spatula to coat. 3. Partially cover the crock pot. Cook on low for 3½ to 5 hours, stirring twice during cooking time, until the oatmeal and nuts are toasted. 4. Remove the granola from the crock pot and spread on two large baking sheets. Add the dried blueberries and cherries to the granola and stir gently. 5. Let the granola cool, then store in an airtight container at room temperature up to one week.

Apple French Toast Bake

Prep time: 20 minutes | Cook time: 5 hours | Serves 8

¼ cup coconut sugar

1 teaspoon ground cinnamon

¼ teaspoon ground cardamom

10 slices whole-wheat bread, cubed

2 Granny Smith apples, peeled

and diced

8 eggs

1 cup canned coconut milk

1 cup unsweetened apple juice

2 teaspoons vanilla extract

1 cup granola

1. Grease a 6-quart crock pot with plain vegetable oil. 2. In a small bowl, mix the coconut sugar, cinnamon, and cardamom well. 3. In the crock pot, layer the bread, apples, and coconut sugar mixture. 4. In a large bowl, mix the eggs, coconut milk, apple juice, and vanilla, and mix well. Pour this mixture slowly over the food in the crock pot. Sprinkle the granola on top. 5. Cover and cook on low for 4 to 5 hours, or until a food thermometer registers 165°F (74°C). 6. Scoop the mixture from the crock pot to serve.

Maple, Apple, and Walnut Great Grains

Prep time: 10 minutes | Cook time: 3 to 4 hours |
Serves 4 to 6

2 large apples
½ cup quinoa, rinsed
½ cup steel-cut oats
½ cup wheat berries
½ cup pearl barley
½ cup bulgur wheat
1 tablespoon ground flaxseed
2 teaspoons ground cinnamon

½ teaspoon ground or grated nutmeg
7 cups water
⅓ cup maple syrup (optional)
½ cup chopped walnuts
½ cup raisins
Unsweetened plant-based milk, for serving (optional)

1. Peel, core, and chop the apples and place them in the crock pot. Add the quinoa, oats, wheat berries, barley, bulgur wheat, flaxseed, cinnamon, nutmeg, water, and maple syrup (if using). Stir gently. Cover and cook on High for 3 to 4 hours or on Low for 7 to 8 hours. 2. Before serving, stir in the walnuts and raisins. Spoon into a bowl and add your favorite milk (if using).

Protein Oatmeal Bake

Prep time: 5 minutes | Cook time: 6 to 8 hours |
Serves 8

Nonstick cooking spray
2 cups steel-cut oats
2 teaspoons protein powder
1 teaspoon baking powder
1 teaspoon ground cinnamon
½ teaspoon salt

2 cups almond milk
¼ cup honey
1 ripe banana, mashed
1 large egg
1 tablespoon pure vanilla extract

1. Spray the crock pot generously with nonstick cooking spray. 2. In a large bowl, mix together the oats, protein powder, baking powder, cinnamon, salt, milk, honey, banana, egg, and vanilla. Pour the mixture into the crock pot. 3. Cook on low for 6 to 8 hours, or until the oatmeal is set, and serve.

Egg and Potato Strata

Prep time: 20 minutes | Cook time: 8 hours | Serves 8

8 Yukon Gold potatoes, peeled and diced
1 onion, minced
2 red bell peppers, stemmed, seeded, and minced
3 Roma tomatoes, seeded and chopped

3 garlic cloves, minced
1½ cups shredded Swiss cheese
8 eggs
2 egg whites
1 teaspoon dried marjoram leaves
1 cup 2% milk

1. In a 6-quart crock pot, layer the diced potatoes, onion, bell peppers, tomatoes, garlic, and cheese. 2. In a medium bowl, mix the eggs, egg whites, marjoram, and milk well with a wire whisk. Pour this mixture into the crock pot. 3. Cover and cook on low for 6 to 8 hours, or until a food thermometer registers 165°F (74°C) and the potatoes are tender. 4. Scoop out of the crock pot to serve.

German Chocolate Cake Protein Oats

Prep time: 15 minutes | Cook time: 6 to 8 hours |
Serves 4 to 6

1 tablespoon coconut oil
2 cups rolled oats
2½ cups water
2 cups full-fat coconut milk
¼ cup unsweetened cacao powder

2 tablespoons collagen peptides
¼ teaspoon sea salt
2 tablespoons pecans
2 tablespoons unsweetened shredded coconu

1. Coat the crock pot with the coconut oil. 2. In your crock pot, combine the oats, water, coconut milk, cacao powder, collagen peptides, and salt. Stir to combine. 3. Cover the cooker and set to low. Cook for 6 to 8 hours. 4. Sprinkle the pecans and coconut on top and serve.

Chapter 2 Poultry

Chicken with Tropical Barbecue Sauce

Prep time: 5 minutes | Cook time: 3 to 9 hours |
Serves 6

¼ cup molasses
2 tablespoons cider vinegar
2 tablespoons Worcestershire sauce
2 teaspoons prepared mustard

⅛ to ¼ teaspoon hot pepper sauce
2 tablespoons orange juice
3 whole chicken breasts, halved

1. Combine molasses, vinegar, Worcestershire sauce, mustard, hot pepper sauce, and orange juice. Brush over chicken. 2. Place chicken in crock pot. 3. Cover. Cook on low 7 to 9 hours, or on high 3 to 4 hours.

Tender Turkey Breast

Prep time: 5 minutes | Cook time: 2 to 9 hours |
Serves 10

1 (6-pound / 2.7-kg) boneless or bone-in turkey breast
2 to 3 tablespoons water

1. Place the turkey breast in the crock pot. Add water. 2. Cover and cook on high 2 to 4 hours, or on low 4 to 9 hours, or until tender but not dry and mushy. 3. Turn over once during cooking time. 4. If you'd like to brown the turkey, place it in your oven and bake it uncovered at 325ºF (165ºC) for 15 to 20 minutes after it's finished cooking in the crock pot.

Reuben Chicken Casserole

Prep time: 30 minutes | Cook time: 4 hours | Serves 6

2 (16-ounce / 454-g) cans sauerkraut, rinsed and drained, divided
1 cup Light Russian salad dressing, divided
6 boneless, skinless chicken

breast halves, divided
1 tablespoon prepared mustard, divided
6 slices Swiss cheese
Fresh parsley for garnish (optional)

1. Place half the sauerkraut in the crock pot. Drizzle with ⅓ cup dressing. 2. Top with 3 chicken breast halves. Spread half the mustard on top of the chicken. 3. Top with remaining sauerkraut and chicken breasts. Drizzle with another ⅓ cup dressing. (Save the remaining dressing until serving time.) 4. Cover and cook on low for 4 hours, or until the chicken is tender, but not dry or mushy. 5. To serve, place a breast half on each of 6 plates. Divide the sauerkraut over the chicken. Top each with a slice of cheese and a drizzle of the remaining dressing. Garnish with parsley if you wish, just before serving.

Thai Chicken

Prep time: 5 minutes | Cook time: 8 to 9 hours |
Serves 6

6 skinless chicken thighs
¾ cup salsa, your choice of heat
¼ cup chunky peanut butter
1 tablespoon low-sodium soy sauce
2 tablespoons lime juice

1 teaspoon grated ginger root (optional)
2 tablespoons chopped cilantro (optional)
1 tablespoon chopped dry-roasted peanuts (optional)

1. Put chicken in crock pot. 2. In a bowl, mix remaining ingredients together, except cilantro and chopped peanuts. 3. Cover and cook on low 8 to 9 hours, or until chicken is cooked through but not dry. 4. Skim off any fat. Remove chicken to a platter and serve topped with sauce. Sprinkle with peanuts and cilantro, if you wish. 5. Serve.

Chicken and Vegetables

Prep time: 15 minutes | Cook time: 6 hours | Serves 4

1 (2.9-ounce / 82-g) packages dry bearnaise sauce mix
½ cup dry white wine
1 pound (454 g) boneless, skinless chicken breasts, cut into bite-sized cubes
1 (9-ounce / 255-g) package frozen mixed vegetables
1 pound (454 g) cooked ham,

cubed
1 pound (454 g) red potatoes, cubed
1 red bell pepper, chopped
1 green bell pepper, chopped
3 shallots, minced
½ teaspoon garlic powder
½ teaspoon turmeric powder
½ teaspoon dried tarragon

1. Combine all ingredients in crock pot. 2. Cover. Cook on low 6 hours.

Easy Mushroom Chicken

Prep time: 10 minutes | Cook time: 3 to 8 hours | Serves 4 to 6

4 to 6 chicken legs and thighs (joined), skinned
Salt and pepper to taste
½ cup chicken broth or dry white wine

1 (10¾-ounce / 305-g) can cream of mushroom or celery soup
1 (4-ounce / 113-g) can sliced mushrooms, drained

1. Sprinkle salt and pepper on each piece of chicken. Place chicken in crock pot. 2. In a small bowl, mix broth and soup together. Pour over chicken. 3. Spoon mushrooms over top. 4. Cover and cook on low 6 to 8 hours, or on high 3 to 4 hours, or until chicken is tender but not dry.

Another Chicken in a Pot

Prep time: 10 minutes | Cook time: 3½ to 10 hours | Serves 4 to 6

1 (1-pound / 454-g) bag baby carrots
1 small onion, diced
1 (14½-ounce / 411-g) can green beans
1 (3-pound / 1.4-kg) whole chicken, cut into serving-size

pieces
2 teaspoons salt
½ teaspoon black pepper
½ cup chicken broth
¼ cup white wine
½ to 1 teaspoon dried basil

1. Put carrots, onion, and beans on bottom of crock pot. Add chicken. Top with salt, pepper, broth, and wine. Sprinkle with basil. 2. Cover. Cook on low 8 to 10 hours, or on high 3½ to 5 hours.

Scalloped Chicken with Stuffing

Prep time: 10 minutes | Cook time: 2 to 3 hours | Serves 4 to 6

4 cups cooked chicken
1 box stuffing mix for chicken
2 eggs

1 cup water
1½ cups milk
1 cup frozen peas

1. Combine chicken and dry stuffing mix. Place in crock pot. 2. Beat eggs, water, and milk together in a bowl. Pour over chicken and stuffing. 3. Cover. Cook on high 2 to 3 hours. 4. Add frozen peas during last hour of cooking.

Chicken, Sweet Chicken

Prep time: 15 minutes | Cook time: 5 to 6 hours | Serves 6 to 8

2 medium raw sweet potatoes, peeled and cut into ¼-inch thick slices
8 boneless, skinless chicken thighs

1 (8-ounce / 227-g) jar orange marmalade
¼ cup water
¼ to ½ teaspoon salt
½ teaspoon pepper

1. Place sweet potato slices in crock pot. 2. Rinse and dry chicken pieces. Arrange on top of the potatoes. 3. Spoon marmalade over the chicken and potatoes. 4. Pour water over all. Season with salt and pepper. 5. Cover and cook on high 1 hour, and then turn to low and cook 4 to 5 hours, or until potatoes and chicken are both tender.

Turkey Meat Loaf

Prep time: 15 minutes | Cook time: 6 to 8 hours | Serves 8

1½ pounds (680 g) lean ground turkey
2 egg whites
⅓ cup ketchup
1 tablespoon Worcestershire sauce
1 teaspoon dried basil

½ teaspoon salt
½ teaspoon black pepper
2 small onions, chopped
2 potatoes, finely shredded
2 small red bell peppers, finely chopped

1. Combine all ingredients in a large bowl. 2. Shape into a loaf to fit in your crock pot. Place in crock pot. 3. Cover. Cook on low 6 to 8 hours.

One-Dish Chicken Supper

Prep time: 5 minutes | Cook time: 6 to 8 hours | Serves 4

4 boneless, skinless chicken breast halves
1 (10¾-ounce / 305-g) can cream of chicken or celery or mushroom soup

⅓ cup milk
1 package Stove Top stuffing mix and seasoning packet
1⅔ cups water

1. Place chicken in crock pot. 2. Combine soup and milk. Pour over chicken. 3. Combine stuffing mix, seasoning packet, and water. Spoon over chicken. 4. Cover. Cook on low 6 to 8 hours.

Delicious Chicken

Prep time: 10 minutes | Cook time: 8 to 10 hours | Serves 6

3 whole chicken breasts, skin removed and halved
1 (10¾-ounce / 305-g) can low-sodium condensed cream of chicken soup
½ cup cooking sherry
1 (4-ounce / 113-g) can sliced
mushrooms, drained
1 teaspoon Worcestershire sauce
1 teaspoon dried tarragon leaves or dried rosemary
¼ teaspoon garlic powder

1. Rinse chicken breasts and pat dry. Place in crock pot. 2. Combine remaining ingredients and pour over chicken breasts, making sure that all pieces are glazed with the sauce. 3. Cover and cook on low 8 to 10 hours, or on high 4 to 5 hours. 4. Serve.

Low-Fat Chicken Cacciatore

Prep time: 15 minutes | Cook time: 8 hours | Serves 10

2 pounds (907 g) uncooked boneless, skinless chicken breasts, cubed
½ pound (227 g) fresh mushrooms
1 bell pepper, chopped
1 medium-sized onion, chopped
1 (12-ounce / 340-g) can low-sodium chopped tomatoes
1 (6-ounce / 170-g) can low-sodium tomato paste
1 (12-ounce / 340-g) can low-sodium tomato sauce
½ teaspoon dried oregano
½ teaspoon dried basil
½ teaspoon garlic powder
½ teaspoon salt
½ teaspoon black pepper

1. Combine all ingredients in crock pot. 2. Cover. Cook on low 8 hours. 3. Serve.

Wild Rice Hot Dish

Prep time: 15 minutes | Cook time: 4 to 6 hours | Serves 8 to 10

2 cups wild rice, uncooked
½ cup slivered almonds
½ cup chopped onions
½ cup chopped celery
8 to 12 ounces (227 to 340 g) can mushrooms, drained
2 cups cooked, cut-up chicken
6 cups chicken broth
¼-½ teaspoon salt
¼ teaspoon pepper
¼ teaspoon garlic powder
1 tablespoon chopped parsley

1. Wash and drain rice. 2. Combine all ingredients in crock pot. Mix well. 3. Cover. Cook on low 4 to 6 hours, or until rice is finished. Do not remove lid before rice has cooked 4 hours.

Chicken Azteca

Prep time: 20 minutes | Cook time: 2½ to 6½ hours | Serves 10 to 12

2 (15-ounce / 425-g) cans black beans, drained
4 cups frozen corn kernels
2 garlic cloves, minced
¾ teaspoon ground cumin
2 cups chunky salsa, divided
10 skinless, boneless chicken breast halves
2 (8-ounce / 227-g) packages cream cheese, cubed
Rice, cooked
Shredded Cheddar cheese

1. Combine beans, corn, garlic, cumin, and half of salsa in crock pot. 2. Arrange chicken breasts over top. Pour remaining salsa over top. 3. Cover. Cook on high 2 to 3 hours, or on low 4 to 6 hours. 4. Remove chicken and cut into bite-sized pieces. Return to cooker. 5. Stir in cream cheese. Cook on high until cream cheese melts. 6. Spoon chicken and sauce over cooked rice. Top with shredded cheese.

Chicken in a Hurry

Prep time: 10 minutes | Cook time: 4 to 8 hours | Serves 4 to 5

2½ to 3 pounds (1.1 to 1.4 kg) skinless chicken drumsticks
½ cup ketchup
¼ cup water
¼ cup brown sugar
1 package dry onion soup mix

1. Arrange chicken in crock pot. 2. Combine remaining ingredients. Pour over chicken. 3. Cover. Cook on high 4 to 5 hours, or on low 7 to 8 hours.

crock pot Stuffing with Poultry

Prep time: 15 minutes | Cook time: 7 to 9 hours | Serves 18

1 large loaf dried low-fat bread, cubed
2 cups chopped, cooked turkey or chicken, skin removed
1 large onion, chopped
3 ribs celery with leaves, chopped
¼ cup butter, melted
4 cups fat-free chicken broth
1 tablespoon poultry seasoning
1 teaspoon salt
4 eggs, beaten
½ teaspoon black pepper

1. Mix together all ingredients. Pour into crock pot. 2. Cover and cook on high 1 hour, then reduce to low 6 to 8 hours.

Cape Breton Chicken

Prep time: 15 minutes | Cook time: 7 hours | Serves 5

4 boneless, skinless chicken breast halves, uncooked, cubed
1 medium onion, chopped
1 medium green bell pepper, chopped
1 cup chopped celery
1 quart low-sodium stewed or

crushed tomatoes
1 cup water
½ cup tomato paste
2 tablespoons Worcestershire sauce
2 tablespoons brown sugar
1 teaspoon black pepper

1. Combine all ingredients in crock pot. 2. Cover. Cook on low 7 hours. 3. Serve.

Maple-Glazed Turkey Breast with Rice

Prep time: 15 minutes | Cook time: 4 to 6 hours | Serves 4

1 (6-ounce / 170-g) package long-grain wild rice mix
1½ cups water
1 (2-pound / 907-g) boneless turkey breast, cut into 1½ to

2-inch chunks
¼ cup maple syrup
1 onion, chopped
¼ teaspoon ground cinnamon
½ teaspoon salt (optional)

1. Combine all ingredients in the crock pot. 2. Cook on low 4 to 6 hours, or until turkey and rice are both tender, but not dry or mushy.

Convenient Chicken and Dumplings

Prep time: 10 minutes | Cook time: 2½ hours | Serves 5 to 6

1 pound (454 g) boneless, skinless chicken breasts, uncooked and cut in 1-inch cubes
1 pound (454 g) frozen vegetables of your choice

1 medium onion, diced
2 (12-ounce / 340-g) jars fat-free low-sodium chicken broth, divided
1½ cups low-fat buttermilk biscuit mix

1. Combine chicken, vegetables, onion, and chicken broth (reserve ½ cup, plus 1 tablespoon, broth) in crock pot. 2. Cover. Cook on high 2 hours. 3. Mix biscuit mix with reserved broth until moistened. Drop by tablespoonfuls over hot chicken and vegetables. 4. Cover. Cook on high 10 minutes. 5. Uncover. Cook on high 20 minutes more.

Chicken and Rice

Prep time: 10 minutes | Cook time: 5 to 6 hours | Serves 6

1 (10¾-ounce / 305-g) can cream of chicken soup
1 package dry onion soup mix
2½ cups water

1 cup long-grain rice, uncooked
6 ounces (170 g) boneless, skinless chicken breast tenders
¼ teaspoon black pepper

1. Combine all ingredients in crock pot. 2. Cook on low 5 to 6 hours. 3. Stir occasionally.

Chicken and Shrimp Casserole

Prep time: 20 minutes | Cook time: 3 to 8 hours | Serves 6

1¼ cups rice, uncooked
2 tablespoons butter, melted
3 cups fat-free, low-sodium chicken broth
1 cup water
3 cups cut-up, cooked skinless chicken breast
2 (4-ounce / 113-g) cans sliced

mushrooms, drained
⅓ cup light soy sauce
1 (12-ounce / 340-g) package shelled frozen shrimp
8 green onions, chopped, 2 tablespoons reserved
⅔ cup slivered almonds

1. Combine rice and butter in crock pot. Stir to coat rice well. 2. Add remaining ingredients except almonds and 2 tablespoons green onions. 3. Cover. Cook on low 6 to 8 hours, or on high 3 to 4 hours, until rice is tender. 4. Sprinkle almonds and green onions over top before serving.

Can-You-Believe-It's-So-Simple Salsa Chicken

Prep time: 5 minutes | Cook time: 5 to 8 hours | Serves 4 to 6

4 to 6 boneless, skinless chicken breast halves
1 (16-ounce / 454-g) jar chunky-style salsa, your choice

of heat
2 cups shredded cheese, your choice of flavor

1. Place chicken in crock pot. Pour salsa over chicken. 2. Cover and cook on low 5 to 8 hours, or until chicken is tender but not dry. 3. Top individual servings with shredded cheese and serve.

Chicken Divan

Prep time: 15 minutes | Cook time: 3 to 4 hours | Serves 4

4 boneless, skinless chicken breast halves
4 cups chopped broccoli, fresh or frozen
2 (10¾-ounce / 305-g) cans

cream of chicken soup
1 cup mayonnaise
½ to 1 teaspoon curry powder, depending upon your taste preference

1. Place chicken breasts in crock pot. 2. Top with broccoli. 3. In a small mixing bowl, blend soup, mayonnaise, and curry powder together. Pour over top of chicken and broccoli. 4. Cover and cook on high 3 to 4 hours, or until chicken and broccoli are tender but not mushy or dry. Serve.

Slow-Cooked Turkey Dinner

Prep time: 15 minutes | Cook time: 7½ hours | Serves 4 to 6

1 onion, diced
6 small red potatoes, quartered
2 cups sliced carrots
1½ to 2 pounds (680 to 907 g) boneless, skinless turkey thighs
¼ cup flour

2 tablespoons dry onion soup mix
1 (10¾-ounce / 305-g) can cream of mushroom soup
⅔ cup chicken broth or water

1. Place vegetables in bottom of crock pot. 2. Place turkey thighs over vegetables. 3. Combine remaining ingredients. Pour over turkey. 4. Cover. Cook on high 30 minutes. Reduce heat to low and cook 7 hours.

Cranberry-Orange Turkey Breast

Prep time: 10 minutes | Cook time: 3½ to 8 hours | Serves 9

½ cup orange marmalade
1 (16-ounce / 454-g) can whole cranberries in sauce

2 teaspoons orange zest, grated
1 (3-pound / 1.4-kg) turkey breast

1. Combine marmalade, cranberries, and zest in a bowl. 2. Place the turkey breast in the crock pot and pour half the orange-cranberry mixture over the turkey. 3. Cover. Cook on low 7 to 8 hours, or on high 3½ to 4 hours, until turkey juices run clear. 4. Add remaining half of orange-cranberry mixture for the last half hour of cooking. 5. Remove turkey to warm platter and allow to rest for 15 minutes before slicing. 6. Serve with orange-cranberry sauce.

Chili Barbecued Chicken Wings

Prep time: 5 minutes | Cook time: 2 to 8 hours | Serves 10

5 pounds (2.3 kg) chicken wings, tips cut off
1 (12-ounce / 340-g) bottle chili sauce
⅓ cup lemon juice
1 tablespoon Worcestershire

sauce
2 tablespoons molasses
1 teaspoon salt
2 teaspoons chili powder
¼ teaspoon hot pepper sauce
Dash garlic powder

1. Place wings in cooker. 2. Combine remaining ingredients and pour over chicken. 3. Cover. Cook on low 6 to 8 hours, or on high 2 to 3 hours.

Healthy Chicken

Prep time: 10 minutes | Cook time: 3½ to 4 hours | Serves 8

3½ pounds (1.6 kg) chicken pieces or whole chicken, cut up
2 cups skim milk
5 cups rice or corn cereal, finely

crushed
1 teaspoon salt
½ teaspoon black pepper

1. Remove skin from chicken. Dip in milk. 2. Put crumbs in a plastic bag. Drop chicken pieces into bag to coat with cereal. Shake well. 3. Place chicken pieces in crock pot. Sprinkle with salt and pepper. 4. Cover. Cook on high 3½ to 4 hours.

Company Casserole

Prep time: 20 minutes | Cook time: 3 to 8 hours | Serves 4 to 6

1¼ cups rice, uncooked
½ cup (1 stick) butter, melted
3 cups chicken broth
3 to 4 cups cut-up cooked chicken breast
2 (4-ounce / 113-g) cans sliced mushrooms, drained

⅓ cup soy sauce
1 (12-ounce / 340-g) package shelled frozen shrimp
8 green onions, chopped, 2 tablespoons reserved
⅔ cup slivered almonds

1. Combine rice and butter in crock pot. Stir to coat rice well. 2. Add remaining ingredients except almonds and 2 tablespoons green onions. 3. Cover. Cook on low 6 to 8 hours, or on high 3 to 4 hours, until rice is tender. 4. Sprinkle almonds and green onions over top before serving.

Chicken and Sausage Cacciatore

Prep time: 35 minutes | Cook time: 8 hours | Serves 4 to 6

1 large green pepper, sliced in 1-inch strips
1 cup sliced mushrooms
1 medium onion, sliced in rings
1 pound (454 g) skinless, boneless chicken breasts, browned

1 pound (454 g) Italian sausage, browned
½ teaspoon dried oregano
½ teaspoon dried basil
1½ cups Italian-style tomato sauce

1. Layer vegetables in crock pot. 2. Top with meat. 3. Sprinkle with oregano and basil. 4. Top with tomato sauce. 5. Cover. Cook on low 8 hours. 6. Remove cover during last 30 minutes of cooking time to allow sauce to cook off and thicken. 7. Serve.

Curried Chicken Dinner

Prep time: 20 minutes | Cook time: 5 to 10 hours | Serves 6

1½ pounds (680 g) boneless, skinless chicken thighs, quartered
3 potatoes, peeled and cut into chunks
1 apple, chopped

2 tablespoons curry powder
1 (14½-ounce / 411-g) can chicken broth
1 medium onion, chopped (optional)

1. Place all ingredients in crock pot. Mix together gently. 2. Cover and cook on low 8 to 10 hours, or on high 5 hours, or until chicken is tender but not dry. 3. Serve.

Creamy Italian Chicken

Prep time: 10 minutes | Cook time: 4 hours | Serves 4

4 boneless, skinless chicken breast halves
1 envelope dry Italian salad dressing mix
¼ cup water
1 (8-ounce / 227-g) package

cream cheese, softened
1 (10¾-ounce / 305-g) can cream of chicken or celery soup
1 (4-ounce / 113-g) can mushroom stems and pieces, drained (optional)

1. Place chicken in crock pot. Combine salad dressing and water. Pour over chicken. 2. Cover and cook on low 3 hours. 3. In a small bowl, beat cream cheese and soup until blended. Stir in mushrooms if you wish. Pour over chicken. 4. Cover and cook on low 1 hour, or until chicken is tender but not dry.

Gran's Big Potluck

Prep time: 20 minutes | Cook time: 10 to 12 hours | Serves 10 to 15

2½ to 3 pounds (1.1 to 1.4 kg) stewing hen, cut into pieces
½ pound (227 g) stewing beef, cubed
1 (½-pound / 227-g) veal shoulder or roast, cubed
1½ quarts water
½ pound (227 g) small red potatoes, cubed
½ pound (227 g) small onions, cut in half
1 cup sliced carrots
1 cup chopped celery
1 green pepper, chopped

1 (1-pound / 454-g) package frozen lima beans
1 cup fresh or frozen okra
1 cup whole-kernel corn
1 (8-ounce / 227-g) can whole tomatoes with juice
1 (15-ounce / 425-g) can tomato purée
1 teaspoon salt
¼ to ½ teaspoon pepper
1 teaspoon dry mustard
½ teaspoon chili powder
¼ cup chopped fresh parsley

1. Combine all ingredients except last 5 seasonings in one very large crock pot, or divide between two medium-sized ones. 2. Cover. Cook on low 10 to 12 hours. Add seasonings during last hour of cooking.

Savory Turkey Meatballs in Italian Sauce

Prep time: 30 minutes | Cook time: 6 to 8 hours | Serves 8

1 (28-ounce / 794-g) can crushed tomatoes
1 tablespoon red wine vinegar
1 medium onion, finely chopped
2 garlic cloves, minced
¼ teaspoon Italian herb seasoning
1 teaspoon dried basil
1 pound (454 g) ground turkey

⅛ teaspoon garlic powder
⅛ teaspoon black pepper
⅓ cup dried parsley
2 egg whites
¼ teaspoon dried minced onion
⅓ cup quick oats
¼ cup grated Parmesan cheese
¼ cup flour
Oil

1. Combine tomatoes, vinegar, onions, garlic, Italian seasonings, and basil in crock pot. Turn to low. 2. Combine remaining ingredients, except flour and oil. Form into 1-inch balls. Dredge each ball in flour. Brown in oil in skillet over medium heat. Transfer to crock pot. Stir into sauce. 3. Cover. Cook on low 6 to 8 hours. 4. Serve.

Sweet Aromatic Chicken

Prep time: 5 minutes | Cook time: 5 to 6 hours |

Serves 6 to 8

½ cup coconut milk
½ cup water
8 chicken thighs, skinned
½ cup brown sugar

2 tablespoons soy sauce
⅛ teaspoon ground cloves
2 garlic cloves, minced

1. Combine coconut milk and water. Pour into greased crock pot. 2. Add remaining ingredients in order listed. 3. Cover. Cook on low 5 to 6 hours.

Barbecued Chicken Breasts

Prep time: 10 minutes | Cook time: 3 to 8 hours |

Serves 8

8 boneless, skinless chicken
breast halves
1 (8-ounce / 227-g) can low-sodium tomato sauce
1 (8-ounce / 227-g) can water
2 tablespoons brown sugar
2 tablespoons prepared mustard
2 tablespoons Worcestershire

sauce
¼ cup cider vinegar
½ teaspoon salt
¼ teaspoon black pepper
Dash of garlic powder
Dash of dried oregano
3 tablespoons onion, chopped
Nonfat cooking spray

1. Place chicken in crock pot sprayed with nonfat cooking spray. Overlap chicken as little as possible. 2. Combine remaining ingredients. Pour over chicken. 3. Cover. Cook on low 6 to 8 hours, or on high 3 to 4 hours. 4. To thicken the sauce a bit, remove the lid during the last hour of cooking.

Herby Barbecued Chicken

Prep time: 10 minutes | Cook time: 6 to 8 hours |

Serves 4 to 6

1 whole chicken, cut up, or 8 of
your favorite pieces
1 onion, thinly sliced
1 bottle Sweet Baby Ray's

Barbecue Sauce
1 teaspoon dried oregano
1 teaspoon dried basil

1. Place chicken in crock pot. 2. Mix onion slices, sauce, oregano, and basil together in a bowl. Pour over chicken, covering as well as possible. 3. Cover and cook on low 6 to 8 hours, or until chicken is tender but not dry.

Chicken Vegetable Gala

Prep time: 15 minutes | Cook time: 6 to 8 hours |

Serves 4

4 bone-in chicken breast halves
1 small head of cabbage,
quartered
1 (1-pound / 454-g) package

baby carrots
2 (14½-ounce / 411-g) cans
Mexican-flavored stewed
tomatoes

1. Place all ingredients in crock pot in order listed. 2. Cover and cook on low 6 to 8 hours, or until chicken and vegetables are tender.

Noodleless Lasagna

Prep time: 20 minutes | Cook time: 4 to 4½ hours |

Serves 4

1½ pounds (680 g) fat-free
ground turkey
1½ cups meat-free, low-sodium
spaghetti sauce
8 ounces (227 g) sliced
mushrooms
1½ cups fat-free ricotta cheese

1 egg, beaten
1 cup shredded Mozzarella
cheese (part skim), divided
1½ teaspoons Italian seasoning
10 slices turkey pepperoni
Nonfat cooking spray

1. Brown ground turkey in a nonstick skillet. 2. Add spaghetti sauce and mushrooms and mix with meat. 3. Pour half of turkey mixture into crock pot sprayed with nonfat cooking spray. 4. In a small bowl, mix together the ricotta cheese, egg, ¼ cup of Mozzarella, and the Italian seasoning. Beat well with a fork. 5. Lay half of pepperoni slices on top of turkey mixture. 6. Spread half of cheese mixture over pepperoni. 7. Repeat layers, finishing by sprinkling the remaining Mozzarella on top. 8. Cover. Cook on low 4 to 4½ hours.

Loretta's Hot Chicken

Prep time: 15 minutes | Cook time: 2 hours | Serves 12

8 cups cubed cooked chicken or
turkey
1 medium onion, chopped

1 cup chopped celery
2 cups mayonnaise
1 cup cubed American cheese

1. Combine all ingredients except buns in crock pot. 2. Cover. Cook on high 2 hours. 3. Serve.

Chicken in Mushroom Sauce

Prep time: 15 minutes | Cook time: 4 to 5 hours | Serves 4

4 boneless, skinless chicken breast halves
1 (10¾-ounce / 305-g) can cream of mushroom soup
1 cup sour cream
1 (7-ounce / 198-g) can

mushroom stems and pieces, drained (optional)
4 bacon strips, cooked and crumbled, or ¼ cup precooked bacon crumbles

1. Place chicken in crock pot. 2. In a mixing bowl, combine soup and sour cream, and mushroom pieces if you wish. Pour over chicken. 3. Cover and cook on low 4 to 5 hours, or until chicken is tender, but not dry. 4. Sprinkle with bacon before serving. 5. Serve.

Garlic-Lime Chicken

Prep time: 10 minutes | Cook time: 4 to 8 hours | Serves 5

5 chicken breast halves
½ cup soy sauce
¼ to ⅓ cup lime juice, according to your taste preference
1 tablespoon Worcestershire

sauce
2 garlic cloves, minced, or 1 teaspoon garlic powder
½ teaspoon dry mustard
½ teaspoon ground pepper

1. Place chicken in crock pot. 2. Combine remaining ingredients and pour over chicken. 3. Cover. Cook on high 4 to 6 hours, or on low 6 to 8 hours.

Scalloped Chicken with Potatoes

Prep time: 5 minutes | Cook time: 4 to 10 hours | Serves 4

1 (5-ounce / 142-g) package scalloped potatoes
Scalloped potatoes dry seasoning pack
4 chicken breast halves or 8

legs
1 (10-ounce / 283-g) package frozen peas
2 cups water

1. Put potatoes, seasoning pack, chicken, and peas in crock pot. Pour water over all. 2. Cover. Cook on low 8 to 10 hours, or on high 4 hours.

Chicken and Apples

Prep time: 20 minutes | Cook time: 7 to 8 hours | Serves 6

1 (6-ounce / 170-g) can frozen orange concentrate, thawed
½ teaspoon dried marjoram leaves
Dash ground nutmeg
Dash garlic powder
1 onion, chopped

6 skinless, boneless chicken breast halves
3 Granny Smith apples, cored and sliced
¼ cup water
2 tablespoons cornstarch

1. In a small bowl, combine orange juice concentrate, marjoram, nutmeg, and garlic powder. 2. Place onions in bottom of crock pot. 3. Dip each chicken breast into the orange mixture to coat. Then place in crock pot over onions. 4. Pour any remaining orange juice concentrate mixture over the chicken. 5. Cover. Cook on low 6 to 7 hours. 6. Add apples and cook on low 1 hour longer. 7. Remove chicken, apples, and onions to a serving platter. 8. Pour the sauce that remains into a medium saucepan. 9. Mix together water and cornstarch. Stir into the juices. 10. Cook over medium heat, stirring constantly until the sauce is thick and bubbly. 11. Serve the sauce over the chicken.

Southern Barbecue Spaghetti Sauce

Prep time: 20 minutes | Cook time: 4 to 5 hours | Serves 12

1 pound (454 g) lean ground turkey
2 medium onions, chopped
1½ cups sliced fresh mushrooms
1 medium green bell pepper, chopped
2 garlic cloves, minced
1 (14½-ounce / 411-g) can diced tomatoes, undrained
1 (12-ounce / 340-g) can tomato

paste
1 (8-ounce / 227-g) can tomato sauce
1 cup ketchup
½ cup fat-free beef broth
2 tablespoons Worcestershire sauce
2 tablespoons brown sugar
1 tablespoon ground cumin
2 teaspoons chili powder
12 cups spaghetti, cooked

1. In a large nonstick skillet, cook the turkey, onions, mushrooms, green pepper, and garlic over medium heat until meat is no longer pink. Drain. 2. Transfer to crock pot. Stir in tomatoes, tomato paste, tomato sauce, ketchup, broth, Worcestershire sauce, brown sugar, cumin, and chili powder. Mix well. 3. Cook on low 4 to 5 hours. Serve over spaghetti.

Chicken Gumbo

Prep time: 25 minutes | Cook time: 3 to 10 hours |
Serves 6 to 8

1 large onion, chopped

3 to 4 garlic cloves, minced

1 green pepper, diced

2 cups okra, sliced

2 cups tomatoes, chopped

4 cups chicken broth

1 pound (454 g) chicken breast, cut into 1-inch pieces

2 teaspoons Old Bay Seasoning

1. Combine all ingredients in crock pot. 2. Cover. Cook on low 8 to 10 hours, or on high 3 to 4 hours. 3. Serve.

Chicken and Shrimp Jambalaya

Prep time: 15 minutes | Cook time: 2¼ to 3¾ hours |
Serves 5 to 6

1 (3½- to 4-pound / 1.6- to 1.8-kg) roasting chicken, cut up

3 onions, diced

1 carrot, sliced

3 to 4 garlic cloves, minced

1 teaspoon dried oregano

1 teaspoon dried basil

1 teaspoon salt

⅛ teaspoon white pepper

1 (14-ounce / 397-g) crushed tomatoes

1 pound (454 g) shelled raw shrimp

2 cups rice, cooked

1. Combine all ingredients except shrimp and rice in crock pot. 2. Cover. Cook on low 2 to 3½ hours, or until chicken is tender. 3. Add shrimp and rice. 4. Cover. Cook on high 15 to 20 minutes, or until shrimp are done.

Curried Chicken with Apples

Prep time: 15 minutes | Cook time: 6 to 7 hours |
Serves 7

1½ pounds (680 g) uncooked boneless skinless chicken breasts, cubed

2½ cups finely chopped apples

1 (10¾-ounce / 305-g) can 98% fat-free cream of mushroom soup, undiluted

1 (4-ounce / 113-g) can

mushroom pieces

1 medium onion, chopped

½ cup skim milk

2 to 3 teaspoons curry powder, according to your taste preference

¼ teaspoon paprika

1 cup peas, thawed

1. Combine all ingredients except peas in greased crock pot. 2. Cook on low 5 to 6 hours. 3. Add peas. 4. Cook an additional hour. 5. Serve.

Chicken Soft Tacos

Prep time: 5 minutes | Cook time: 6 to 8 hours |
Serves 6

1 to 1½ pounds (680 g) frozen, boneless, skinless chicken breasts

1 (14½-ounce / 411-g) can low-

sodium diced tomatoes with green chilies

1 envelope low-sodium taco seasoning

1. Place chicken breasts in crock pot. 2. Mix tomatoes and taco seasoning. Pour over chicken. 3. Cover. Cook on low 6 to 8 hours. 4. Serve.

Pacific Chicken

Prep time: 10 minutes | Cook time: 7 to 8 hours |
Serves 6

6 to 8 skinless chicken thighs

½ cup soy sauce

2 tablespoons brown sugar

2 tablespoons grated fresh ginger

2 garlic cloves, minced

1. Wash and dry chicken. Place in crock pot. 2. Combine remaining ingredients. Pour over chicken. 3. Cover. Cook on high 1 hour. Reduce heat to low and cook 6 to 7 hours. 4. Serve.

One-Pot Chicken Dinner

Prep time: 15 minutes | Cook time: 3 to 6 hours |
Serves 6

12 chicken drumsticks or thighs, skin removed

3 medium sweet potatoes, cut into 2-inch pieces

1 (12-ounce / 340-g) jar chicken gravy, or 1 (10¾-ounce / 305-g) can cream of chicken soup

2 tablespoons unbleached flour, if using chicken gravy

1 teaspoon dried parsley flakes (optional)

½ teaspoon dried rosemary (optional)

Salt and pepper to taste (optional)

1 (10-ounce / 283-g) package frozen cut green beans

1. Place chicken in crock pot. Top with sweet potatoes chunks. 2. In small bowl, combine remaining ingredients, except beans, and mix until smooth. Pour over chicken. 3. Cover and cook on high 1½ hours, or on low 3½ hours. 4. One and one-half hours before serving, stir green beans into chicken mixture. Cover and cook on low 1 to 2 hours, or until chicken, sweet potatoes, and green beans are tender, but not dry or mushy.

Chicken at a Whim

Prep time: 10 minutes | Cook time: 4½ hours |
Serves 6 to 8

6 medium, boneless, skinless chicken breast halves
1 small onion, sliced
1 cup dry white wine, chicken broth, or water
1 (15-ounce / 425-g) can chicken broth
2 cups water
1 (6-ounce / 170-g) can sliced

black olives, with juice
1 small can artichoke hearts, with juice
5 garlic cloves, minced
1 cup dry elbow macaroni or small shells
1 envelope dry savory garlic soup

1. Place chicken in crock pot. Spread onion over chicken. 2. Combine remaining ingredients, except dry soup mix, and pour over chicken. Sprinkle with dry soup. 3. Cover. Cook on low 4½ hours.

Aloha Chicken Cosmopolitan

Prep time: 15 minutes | Cook time: 6 hours | Serves 12

5 pounds (2.3 kg) boneless, skinless chicken breasts, cut into strips or cubed
Dash of salt

1 cup frozen orange juice 1 cup coconut milk
1 cup soy sauce
¼ cup sesame oil

1. Lightly salt chicken and then refrigerate for 30 minutes. 2. Drain chicken of any juices that have gathered and combine with other ingredients in large crock pot. 3. Cover. Cook on low 6 hours. 4. Serve.

Saucy Turkey Meatballs

Prep time: 20 minutes | Cook time: 6 to 8 hours |
Serves 6

½ pound (227 g) lean ground turkey
1 cup oat bran
1 clove garlic, crushed
2 tablespoons water
1 tablespoon low-sodium soy

sauce
3 egg whites
½ cup onions, diced
½ cup low-sodium chili sauce
½ cup grape jelly
¼ cup Dijon mustard

1. Combine turkey, oat bran, garlic, water, soy sauce, egg whites, and onions. Shape into 24 balls (1 tablespoon per ball). 2. Place meatballs on baking sheet and bake at 350° for 15 to 20 minutes until browned. (They can be made ahead and frozen.) 3. Mix together chili sauce, grape jelly, and Dijon mustard. 4. Combine meatballs and sauce in crock pot. 5. Cover. Cook on low 6 to 8 hours.

Marinated Chinese Chicken Salad

Prep time: 25 minutes | Cook time: 3 to 8 hours |
Serves 8

Marinade:
3 cloves minced garlic
1 tablespoon fresh ginger, grated
1 teaspoon dried red pepper flakes
2 tablespoons honey
3 tablespoons low-sodium soy sauce
6 boneless, skinless chicken breast halves
Dressing:

½ cup rice wine vinegar
1 clove garlic, minced
1 teaspoon fresh grated ginger
1 tablespoon honey
Salad:
1 large head iceberg lettuce, shredded
2 carrots, julienned
½ cup chopped roasted peanuts
¼ cup chopped cilantro
½ package mei fun noodles, fried in hot oil

1. Mix marinade ingredients in a small bowl. 2. Place chicken in crock pot and pour marinade over chicken, coating each piece well. 3. Cover. Cook on low 6 to 8 hours, or on high 3 to 4 hours. 4. Remove chicken from crock pot and cool. Reserve juices. Shred chicken into bite-sized pieces. 5. In a small bowl, combine the dressing ingredients with ½ cup of the juice from the crock pot. 6. In a large serving bowl toss together the shredded chicken, lettuce, carrots, peanuts, cilantro, and noodles. 7. Just before serving, drizzle with the salad dressing. Toss well and serve.

Lemon-Honey Chicken

Prep time: 5 minutes | Cook time: 8 hours | Serves 4
to 6

1 lemon
1 whole roasting chicken, rinsed

½ cup orange juice
½ cup honey

1. Pierce lemon with fork. Place in chicken cavity. Place chicken in crock pot. 2. Combine orange juice and honey. Pour over chicken. 3. Cover. Cook on low 8 hours. Remove lemon and squeeze over chicken. 4. Carve chicken and serve.

Barbecue Chicken for Buns

Prep time: 15 minutes | Cook time: 8 hours | Serves 16 to 20

6 cups diced cooked chicken	2 cups water
2 cups chopped celery	2 tablespoons brown sugar
1 cup chopped onions	4 tablespoons vinegar
1 cup chopped green peppers	2 teaspoons dry mustard
4 tablespoons butter	1 teaspoon pepper
2 cups ketchup	1 teaspoon salt

1. Combine all ingredients in crock pot. 2. Cover. Cook on low 8 hours. 3. Stir chicken until it shreds. 4. Serve.

Chicken a la Fruit

Prep time: 20 minutes | Cook time: 6 to 8 hours | Serves 5 to 6

½ cup crushed pineapple, drained	½ to ¾ teaspoon salt
3 whole peaches, mashed	¼ teaspoon pepper
2 tablespoons lemon juice	1 chicken, cut up
2 tablespoons soy sauce	Nonstick cooking spray

1. Spray crock pot with nonstick cooking spray. 2. Mix pineapple, peaches, lemon juice, soy sauce, and salt and pepper in a large bowl. 3. Dip chicken pieces in sauce and then place in crock pot. Pour remaining sauce over all. 4. Cover and cook on low 6 to 8 hours, or until chicken is tender but not dry.

Savory crock pot Chicken

Prep time: 15 minutes | Cook time: 8 to 10 hours | Serves 4

2½ pounds (1.1 kg) chicken pieces, skinned	2 garlic cloves, minced
1 pound (454 g) fresh tomatoes, chopped, or 1 (15-ounce / 425-g) can stewed tomatoes	1 onion, chopped
	½ cup chicken broth
	1 teaspoon dried thyme
2 tablespoons white wine	1½ teaspoons salt
1 bay leaf	2 cups broccoli, cut into bite-sized pieces
¼ teaspoon pepper	

1. Combine all ingredients except broccoli in crock pot. 2. Cover. Cook on low 8 to 10 hours. 3. Add broccoli 30 minutes before serving.

Easy Chicken

Prep time: 10 minutes | Cook time: 8 hours | Serves 6 to 8

8 to 10 chicken wings or legs and thighs	½ cup sugar
½ cup soy sauce	½ teaspoon Tabasco sauce
	Pinch of ground ginger

1. Place chicken in greased crock pot. 2. Combine remaining ingredients and pour over chicken. 3. Cover. Cook on low 8 hours. 4. Serve.

Chapter 3 Beans and Grains

Barbecued Black Beans with Sweet Potatoes

Prep time: 15 minutes | Cook time: 2 to 4 hours |
Serves 4 to 6

4 large sweet potatoes, peeled and cut into 8 chunks each
1 (15-ounce / 425-g) can black beans, rinsed and drained

1 medium onion, diced
2 ribs celery, sliced
9 ounces (255 g) Sweet Baby Ray's Barbecue Sauce

1. Place sweet potatoes in crock pot. 2. Combine remaining ingredients. Pour over sweet potatoes. 3. Cover. Cook on high 2 to 3 hours, or on low 4 hours.

Barbecued Baked Beans

Prep time: 10 minutes | Cook time: 3 to 4 hours |
Serves 8 to 10

2 (16-ounce / 454-g) cans baked beans, your choice of variety
2 (15-ounce / 425-g) cans kidney or pinto beans, or one of

each, drained
½ cup brown sugar
1 cup ketchup
1 onion, chopped

1. Combine all ingredients in crock pot. Mix well. 2. Cover and cook on low 3 to 4 hours, or until heated through.

Sweet-Sour Bean Trio

Prep time: 10 minutes | Cook time: 6 to 8 hours |
Serves 8

4 slices lean bacon
1 onion, chopped
¼ cup brown sugar
1 teaspoon prepared mustard
1 clove garlic, crushed
½ teaspoon salt
¼ cup vinegar

1 (16-ounce / 454-g) can low-sodium lima beans, drained
1 (16-ounce / 454-g) can low-sodium baked beans, undrained
1 (16-ounce / 454-g) can low-sodium kidney beans, drained

1. Brown bacon in a nonstick skillet. Crumble. Combine bacon, 2

tablespoons drippings from bacon, onion, brown sugar, mustard, garlic, salt, and vinegar. 2. Mix with beans in crock pot. 3. Cover. Cook on low 6 to 8 hours.

Cajun Sausage and Beans

Prep time: 10 minutes | Cook time: 8 hours | Serves
4 to 6

1 pound (454 g) smoked sausage, sliced into ¼-inch pieces
1 (16-ounce / 454-g) can red beans
1 (16-ounce / 454-g) can

crushed tomatoes with green chilies
1 cup chopped celery
Half an onion, chopped
2 tablespoons Italian seasoning
Tabasco sauce to taste

1. Combine all ingredients in crock pot. 2. Cover. Cook on low 8 hours. 3. Serve.

Herbed Lentils and Rice

Prep time: 10 minutes | Cook time: 6 to 8 hours |
Serves 4

2¾ cups reduced-sodium fat-free chicken broth
¾ cup water
¾ cup dry lentils, rinsed
¾ cup onions, chopped
½ cup dry wild rice
½ teaspoon dried basil
¼ teaspoon dried oregano

¼ teaspoon dried thyme
⅛ teaspoon garlic powder
½ teaspoon salt
¼ teaspoon black pepper
1 cup shredded reduced-fat Swiss cheese
Fat-free cooking spray

1. Spray crock pot with fat-free cooking spray. 2. Combine all ingredients except cheese in crock pot. 3. Cook on low 6 to 8 hours, or until lentils and rice are tender. Do not remove lid until it has cooked at least 6 hours. 4. Stir in shredded cheese 5 to 10 minutes before serving.

Chili Boston Baked Beans

Prep time: 15 minutes | Cook time: 6 to 8 hours |
Serves 20

1 cup raisins	bacon
2 small onions, diced	2 (15-ounce / 425-g) cans baked
2 tart apples, diced	beans
1 cup chili sauce	3 teaspoons dry mustard
1 cup chopped ham or crumbled	½ cup sweet pickle relish

1. Mix together all ingredients. 2. Cover. Cook on low 6 to 8 hours.

Mixed crock pot Beans

Prep time: 10 minutes | Cook time: 4 to 5 hours |
Serves 6

1 (16-ounce / 454-g) can kidney beans, drained	frozen, green beans
	4 slices lean turkey bacon,
1 (15½-ounce / 439-g) can baked beans, undrained	browned and crumbled
	½ cup ketchup
1 pint home-frozen, or 1 (1-pound / 454-g) package frozen, lima beans	⅓ cup sugar
	⅓ cup brown sugar
	2 tablespoons vinegar
1 pint home-frozen, or 1 (1-pound / 454-g) package	½ teaspoon salt

1. Combine beans and bacon in crock pot. 2. Stir together remaining ingredients. Add to beans and mix well. 3. Cover. Cook on low 4 to 5 hours.

Arroz con Queso

Prep time: 15 minutes | Cook time: 6 to 9 hours |
Serves 6 to 8

1 (14½-ounce / 411-g) can whole tomatoes, mashed	1 cup cottage cheese
	1 (4¼-ounce / 120-g) can
1 (15-ounce / 425-g) can Mexican style beans, undrained	chopped green chili peppers, drained
1½ cups long-grain rice, uncooked	1 tablespoon oil
	3 garlic cloves, minced
1 cup shredded Monterey Jack cheese	1 teaspoon salt
	1 cup shredded Monterey Jack
1 large onion, finely chopped	cheese

1. Combine all ingredients except final cup of cheese. Pour into well greased crock pot. 2. Cover. Cook on low 6 to 9 hours. 3. Sprinkle with remaining cheese before serving.

Easy Wheat Berries

Prep time: 10 minutes | Cook time: 2 hours | Serves
4 to 6

1 cup wheat berries	broth
1 cup couscous or small pasta like orzo	½ to 1 broth can of water
	½ cup dried raisins
1 (14½-ounce / 411-g) can	

1. Cover wheat berries with water and soak 2 hours before cooking. Drain. Spoon wheat berries into crock pot. 2. Combine with remaining ingredients in crock pot. 3. Cover. Cook on low until liquid is absorbed and berries are soft, about 2 hours.

Herb Rice

Prep time: 5 minutes | Cook time: 4 to 6 hours |
Serves 6

3 chicken bouillon cubes	¼ cup dried parsley, chopped
3 cups water	1 tablespoon butter or
1½ cups long-grain rice, uncooked	margarine
	¼ cup onions, diced
1 teaspoon dried rosemary	½ cup slivered almonds
½ teaspoon dried marjoram	(optional)

1. Mix together chicken bouillon cubes and water. 2. Combine all ingredients in crock pot. 3. Cook on low 4 to 6 hours, or until rice is fully cooked.

Wild Rice Pilaf

Prep time: 10 minutes | Cook time: 3½ to 5 hours |
Serves 6

1½ cups wild rice, uncooked	1 (4-ounce / 113-g) can sliced
½ cup finely chopped onion	mushrooms, drained
1 (14-ounce / 397-g) chicken broth	½ teaspoon dried thyme leaves
	Nonstick cooking spray
2 cups water	

1. Spray crock pot with nonstick cooking spray. 2. Rinse rice and drain well. 3. Combine rice, onion, chicken broth, and water in crock pot. Mix well. 4. Cover and cook on high 3 to 4 hours. 5. Add mushrooms and thyme and stir gently. 6. Cover and cook on low 30 to 60 minutes longer, or until wild rice pops and is tender.

Hometown Spanish Rice

**Prep time: 20 minutes | Cook time: 2 to 4 hours |
Serves 6 to 8**

1 large onion, chopped
1 bell pepper, chopped
1 pound (454 g) bacon, cooked, and broken into bite-size pieces
2 cups long-grain rice, cooked

1 (28-ounce / 794-g) can stewed tomatoes with juice
Grated Parmesan cheese (optional)
Nonstick cooking spray

1. Sauté onion and pepper in a small nonstick frying pan until tender. 2. Spray interior of crock pot with nonstick cooking spray. 3. Combine all ingredients in the crock pot. 4. Cover and cook on low 4 hours, or on high 2 hours, or until heated through. 5. Sprinkle with Parmesan cheese just before serving, if you wish.

Football Bean Serve

**Prep time: 20 minutes | Cook time: 6 to 8 hours |
Serves 12**

1 cup minced onions
2 cups diced celery
2 cups diced carrots
2 (15-ounce / 425-g) cans kidney beans, drained and rinsed
2 (15-ounce / 425-g) cans pinto beans, drained and rinsed

2 (15-ounce / 425-g) cans diced tomatoes
2 cups water
1 tablespoon garlic powder
1 tablespoon parsley flakes
1 tablespoon dried oregano
1 tablespoon ground cumin
1 tablespoon salt

1. Brown turkey with onions in a nonstick skillet over medium heat. Add celery and carrots and cook until just wilted. Place in crock pot. 2. Add remaining ingredients. Stir to combine. 3. Cover. Cook on low 6 to 8 hours. 4. Serve.

Hot Bean Dish without Meat

**Prep time: 10 minutes | Cook time: 3 to 4 hours |
Serves 8 to 10**

1 (16-ounce / 454-g) can kidney beans, drained
1 (15-ounce / 425-g) can lima beans, drained
¼ cup vinegar
2 tablespoons molasses

2 heaping tablespoons brown sugar
2 tablespoons minced onion
Mustard to taste
Tabasco sauce to taste

1. Place beans in crock pot. 2. Combine remaining ingredients. Pour over beans. 3. Cover. Cook on low 3 to 4 hours.

Rice 'n Beans 'n Salsa

**Prep time: 10 minutes | Cook time: 4 to 10 hours |
Serves 6 to 8**

2 (16-ounce / 454-g) cans black or navy beans, drained
1 (14-ounce / 397-g) chicken broth
1 cup long-grain white or

brown rice, uncooked
1 quart salsa, your choice of heat
1 cup water
½ teaspoon garlic powder

1. Combine all ingredients in crock pot. Stir well. 2. Cover and cook on low 8 to 10 hours, or on high 4 hours.

Pineapple Baked Beans

**Prep time: 15 minutes | Cook time: 4 to 8 hours |
Serves 6 to 8**

1 pound (454 g) ground beef
1 (28-ounce / 794-g) can baked beans
1 (8-ounce / 227-g) can pineapple tidbits, drained
1 (4½-ounce / 128-g) can sliced mushrooms, drained

1 large onion, chopped
1 large green pepper, chopped
½ cup barbecue sauce
2 tablespoons soy sauce
1 clove garlic, minced
½ teaspoon salt
¼ teaspoon pepper

1. Brown ground beef in skillet. Drain. Place in crock pot. 2. Stir in remaining ingredients. Mix well. 3. Cover Cook on low 4 to 8 hours, or until bubbly. Serve.

No-Meat Baked Beans

**Prep time: 10 minutes | Cook time: 6½ to 9½ hours |
Serves 8 to 10**

1 pound (454 g) dried navy beans
6 cups water
1 small onion, chopped
¾ cup ketchup

½ cup brown sugar
¾ cup water
1 teaspoon dry mustard
3 tablespoons dark molasses
1 teaspoon salt

1. Soak beans in water overnight in large soup kettle. Cook beans in water until soft, about 1½ hours. Drain, discarding bean water. 2. Stir together all ingredients in crock pot. Mix well. 3. Cover. Cook on low 5 to 8 hours, or until beans are well flavored but not breaking down.

Barbecued Lentils

Prep time: 5 minutes | Cook time: 6 to 8 hours | Serves 8

2 cups barbecue sauce
3½ cups water

1 pound (454 g) dry lentils
1 package vegetarian hot dogs, sliced

1. Combine all ingredients in crock pot. 2. Cover. Cook on low 6 to 8 hours.

Never Fail Rice

Prep time: 5 minutes | Cook time: 2 to 6 hours | Serves 6

1 cup long-grain rice, uncooked
2 cups water

½ teaspoon salt
½ tablespoon butter

1. Combine all ingredients in small crock pot. 2. Cover. Cook on low 4 to 6 hours, or on high 2 to 3 hours, or until rice is just fully cooked. 3. Fluff with a fork. Serve.

Creole Black Beans

Prep time: 15 minutes | Cook time: 8 hours | Serves 6 to 8

¾ pound (340 g) lean smoked sausage, sliced in ¼-inch pieces and browned
3 (15-ounce / 425-g) cans black beans, drained
1½ cups chopped onions
1½ cups chopped green bell peppers
1½ cups chopped celery
4 garlic cloves, minced

2 teaspoons dried thyme
1½ teaspoons dried oregano
1½ teaspoons black pepper
1 chicken bouillon cube
3 bay leaves
1 (8-ounce / 227-g) can tomato sauce
1 cup water

1. Combine all ingredients in crock pot. 2. Cover. Cook on low 8 hours, or on high 4 hours. 3. Remove bay leaves before serving.

Chapter 4 Beef, Pork, and Lamb

Barbecued Cola Steak

Prep time: 15 minutes | Cook time: 5½ to 6½ hours | Serves 24

1 (4-pound / 1.8-kg) round steak, ¾-inch thick, cut into (3-inch) cubes	1 cup cola
	½ cup chopped onion
	2 garlic cloves, minced
2 cups ketchup	Nonstick cooking spray

1. Spray crock pot with nonstick cooking spray. 2. Place beef pieces in cooker. 3. Mix remaining ingredients in a large bowl and pour over meat. 4. Cover and cook on high 5 to 6 hours. 5. About 30 minutes before serving, remove beef from crock pot and shred with 2 forks. Return beef to crock pot and mix well with sauce. 6. Cover and cook on high an additional 20 minutes. 7. Serve.

Slow-Cooked Pork Stew

Prep time: 20 minutes | Cook time: 4 to 6 hours | Serves 8

2 pounds (907 g) lean pork loin, cut into 1-inch cubes	pepper, depending on your taste preferences
½ pound (227 g) baby carrots	1 teaspoon dried thyme
3 large potatoes, cut into 1-inch cubes	1 teaspoon salt
2 parsnips, cut into 1-inch cubes	2½ cups low-sodium canned vegetable juice
2 onions, cut into wedges, slices, or chopped coarsely	2 tablespoons brown sugar
3 garlic cloves, minced	1 tablespoon prepared mustard
1 to 2 teaspoons ground black	4 teaspoons tapioca

1. Place pork in crock pot. 2. Add carrots, potatoes, parsnips, onions, garlic, pepper, thyme, and salt. Mix together well. 3. In a medium bowl, combine vegetable juice, brown sugar, mustard, and tapioca. Pour over meat and vegetables. 4. Cover. Cook on low 6 hours, or on high 4 hours.

Shepherd's Pie

Prep time: 40 minutes | Cook time: 3 hours | Serves 3 to 4

1 pound (454 g) ground pork	1 small onion, chopped
1 tablespoon vinegar	1 (15-ounce / 425-g) can corn, drained
1¼ teaspoons salt, divided	
¼ teaspoon hot pepper	3 large potatoes
1 teaspoon paprika	¼ cup milk
¼ teaspoon dried oregano	1 teaspoon butter
¼ teaspoon black pepper	Dash of pepper
1 teaspoon chili powder	Shredded cheese

1. Combine pork, vinegar, and spices except ¼ teaspoon salt. Cook in skillet until brown. Add onion and cook until onions begin to glaze. Spread in bottom of crock pot. 2. Spread corn over meat. 3. Boil potatoes until soft. Mash with milk, butter, ¼ teaspoon salt, and dash of pepper. Spread over meat and corn. 4. Cover. Cook on low 3 hours. Sprinkle top with cheese a few minutes before serving.

Tamale Casserole

Prep time: 10 minutes | Cook time: 5 to 7 hours | Serves 6 to 8

2 pounds (907 g) frozen meatballs	style corn
	1 cup chopped stuffed green olives
1 (28-ounce / 794-g) can chopped tomatoes	½ teaspoon chili powder (optional)
1 cup yellow cornmeal	
1 (16-ounce / 454-g) can cream-	

1. Microwave frozen meatballs for 4 minutes until thawed. Place in crock pot. Combine remaining ingredients in a mixing bowl. Pour over meatballs and mix well. 2. Cover and cook on high 1 hour. Turn to low and cook 4 to 6 hours. Check after 4 hours of cooking. The casserole is finished when it reaches a "loaf" consistency.

Kielbasa and Cabbage

Prep time: 15 minutes | Cook time: 7 to 8 hours | Serves 6

1 (1½-pound / 680-g) head green cabbage, shredded
2 medium onions, chopped
3 medium red potatoes, peeled and cubed
1 red bell pepper, chopped
2 garlic cloves, minced
⅔ cup dry white wine
1½ pounds (680 g) Polish

kielbasa, cut into 3-inch long links
1 (28-ounce / 794-g) can cut-up tomatoes with juice
1 tablespoon Dijon mustard
¾ teaspoon caraway seeds
½ teaspoon pepper
¾ teaspoon salt

1. Combine all ingredients in crock pot. 2. Cover. Cook on low 7 to 8 hours, or until cabbage is tender.

Poppin' Pork Barbecue

Prep time: 10 minutes | Cook time: 8 hours | Serves 8 to 12

1 (3- to 4-pound / 1.4- to 1.8-kg) pork loin
Salt to taste
Pepper to taste
2 cups cider vinegar

2 teaspoons sugar
½ cup ketchup
Crushed red pepper to taste
Tabasco sauce to taste

1. Sprinkle pork with salt and pepper. Place in crock pot. 2. Pour vinegar over meat. Sprinkle sugar on top. 3. Cover. Cook on low 8 hours. 4. Remove pork from cooker and shred meat. 5. In bowl mix together ketchup, red pepper, Tabasco sauce, and ½ cup vinegar-sugar drippings. Stir in shredded meat. 6. Serve.

Slow-Cooked Round Steak

Prep time: 15 minutes | Cook time: 4 to 5 hours | Serves 4 to 6

1 (1¾-pound / 794-g) round steak
¼ cup flour
2 onions, sliced thickly

1 green pepper, sliced in strips
1 (10¾-ounce / 305-g) can cream of mushroom soup

1. Cut steak into serving-size pieces. Dredge in flour. Brown in a nonstick skillet. 2. Place browned steak in crock pot. Top with onion and pepper slices. 3. Pour soup over all, making sure steak pieces are covered. 4. Cover and cook on low 4 to 5 hours.

Easy Meat Loaf

Prep time: 5 minutes | Cook time: 2 hours | Serves 5 to 6

2 pounds (907 g) ground beef
1 (6¼-ounce / 177-g) package stuffing mix for beef, plus

seasoning
2 eggs, beaten
½ cup ketchup, divided

1. Mix beef, dry stuffing, eggs, and ¼ cup ketchup. 2. Shape into an oval loaf. Place in crock pot. Pour remaining ketchup over top. 3. Cover and cook on high for 2 hours.

Supper-in-a-Dish

Prep time: 20 minutes | Cook time: 4 hours | Serves 8

1 pound (454 g) ground beef, browned and drained
1½ cups sliced raw potatoes
1 cup sliced carrots
1 cup peas
½ cup chopped onions
½ cup chopped celery
¼ cup chopped green peppers

1 teaspoon salt
¼ teaspoon pepper
1 (10¾-ounce / 305-g) can cream of chicken, or mushroom, soup
¼ cup milk
⅔ cup shredded sharp cheese

1. Layer ground beef, potatoes, carrots, peas, onions, celery, green peppers, salt, and pepper in crock pot. 2. Combine soup and milk. Pour over layered ingredients. Sprinkle with cheese. 3. Cover. Cook on high 4 hours.

Noodle Hamburger Dish

Prep time: 20 minutes | Cook time: 3 to 4 hours | Serves 10

1½ pounds (680 g) ground beef, browned and drained
1 green pepper, diced
1 quart whole tomatoes
1 (10¾-ounce / 305-g) can cream of mushroom soup
1 large onion, diced

1½ tablespoons Worcestershire sauce
1 (8-ounce / 227-g) package noodles, uncooked
1 teaspoon salt
¼ teaspoon pepper
1 cup shredded cheese

1. Combine all ingredients except cheese in crock pot. 2. Cover. Cook on high 3 to 4 hours. 3. Sprinkle with cheese before serving.

Barbecued Roast Beef

1 (4-pound / 1.8-kg) beef roast	3 tablespoons Worcestershire
1 cup ketchup	sauce
1 onion, chopped	¾ cup brown sugar
¾ cup water	

1. Place roast in crock pot. 2. In a small bowl, mix together all remaining ingredients except the brown sugar. Pour over roast. 3. Cover and cook on low 6 to 7 hours. Approximately 1 hour before serving, sprinkle with ¾ cup brown sugar.

Savory Tenderloins

Prep time: 25 minutes | Cook time: 3 to 5 hours |
Serves 6 to 8

½ cup sliced celery	1 tablespoon butter
¼ pound (113 g) fresh	2 teaspoons salt
mushrooms, quartered	¼ teaspoon pepper
1 medium onion, sliced	1 tablespoon butter
¼ cup butter, melted	½ cup beef broth
2 (1¼-pound / 567-g) pork	1 tablespoon flour
tenderloins	

1. Placed celery, mushrooms, onion, and ¼ cup melted butter in crock pot. 2. Brown tenderloins in skillet in 1 tablespoon butter. Layer over vegetables in crock pot. 3. Sprinkle with salt and pepper. 4. Combine broth and flour until smooth. Pour over tenderloins. 5. Cover. Cook on high 3 hours, or on low 4 to 5 hours.

Quick and Easy Chili

Prep time: 20 minutes | Cook time: 4 to 5 hours |
Serves 4

1 pound (454 g) ground beef	¼ teaspoon cayenne pepper
1 onion, chopped	½ teaspoon salt
1 (16-ounce / 454-g) can stewed	1 tablespoon chili powder
tomatoes	For Garnish:
1 (11½-ounce / 326-g) can Hot	Sour cream
V-8 juice	Chopped green onions
2 (15-ounce / 425-g) cans pinto	Shredded cheese
beans	Sliced ripe olives

1. Crumble ground beef in microwave-safe casserole. Add onion.

Microwave, covered, on high 15 minutes. Drain. Break meat into pieces. 2. Combine all ingredients except garnish ingredients in crock pot. 3. Cook on low 4 to 5 hours. 4. Garnish with sour cream, chopped green onions, shredded cheese, and sliced ripe olives.

Meal-in-One

Prep time: 25 minutes | Cook time: 4 hours | Serves
6 to 8

2 pounds (907 g) ground beef	1 (16-ounce / 454-g) container
1 onion, diced	sour cream
1 green bell pepper, diced	1 (24-ounce / 680-g) container
1 teaspoon salt	cottage cheese
¼ teaspoon pepper	1 cup Monterey Jack cheese,
1 large bag frozen hash brown	shredded
potatoes	

1. Brown ground beef, onion, and green pepper in skillet. Drain. Season with salt and pepper. 2. In crock pot, layer one-third of the potatoes, meat, sour cream, and cottage cheese. Repeat twice. 3. Cover. Cook on low 4 hours, sprinkling Monterey Jack cheese over top during last hour. 4. Serve.

crock pot Stuffing with Sausage

Prep time: 40 minutes | Cook time: 4 hours | Serves 10

12 cups toasted bread crumbs	1 (8-ounce / 227-g) can sliced
or dressing mix	mushrooms, with liquid
1 pound (454 g) bulk sausage,	¼ cup chopped fresh parsley
browned and drained	2 teaspoons poultry seasoning
¼ to 1 cup butter (enough to	(omit if using dressing mix)
flavor bread)	Dash of pepper
1 cup or more finely chopped	½ teaspoon salt
onions	2 eggs, beaten
1 cup or more finely chopped	4 cups chicken stock
celery	

1. Combine bread crumbs and sausage. 2. Melt butter in skillet. Add onions and celery and sauté until tender. Stir in mushrooms and parsley. Add seasonings. Pour over bread crumbs and mix well. 3. Stir in eggs and chicken stock. 4. Pour into crock pot and cook on high 1 hour, and on low an additional 3 hours.

Italian Sausage Dinner

Prep time: 10 minutes | Cook time: 5 to 10 hours |
Serves 6

1½ pounds (680 g) Italian
sausage, cut in ¾-inch slices
2 tablespoons A-1 steak sauce
1 (28-ounce / 794-g) can diced
Italian-style tomatoes, with

juice
2 chopped green peppers
½ teaspoon red pepper flakes
(optional)
2 cups minute rice, uncooked

1. Place all ingredients, except rice, in crock pot. 2. Cover and cook
on low 7½ to 9½ hours, or on high 4½ hours. 3. Stir in uncooked
rice. Cover and cook an additional 20 minutes on high or low.

Tastes-Like-Turkey

Prep time: 15 minutes | Cook time: 3 to 8 hours |
Serves 6

2 pounds (907 g) hamburger,
browned
1 teaspoon salt
½ teaspoon pepper
2 (10¾-ounce / 305-g) cans
cream of chicken soup

1 (10¾-ounce / 305-g) can
cream of celery soup
4 scant cups milk
1 large package bread stuffing
or large loaf of bread, torn in
pieces

1. Combine all ingredients in large buttered crock pot. 2. Cover.
Cook on high 3 hours, or on low 6 to 8 hours.

Italian Spaghetti Sauce

Prep time: 20 minutes | Cook time: 8 to 9 hours |
Serves 8 to 10

2 pounds (907 g) sausage or
ground beef
3 medium onions, chopped
(about 2¼ cups)
2 cups sliced mushrooms
6 garlic cloves, minced
2 (14½-ounce / 411-g) cans
diced tomatoes, undrained
1 (29-ounce / 822-g) can tomato

sauce
1 (12-ounce / 340-g) can tomato
paste
2 tablespoons dried basil
1 tablespoon dried oregano
1 tablespoon sugar
1 teaspoon salt
½ teaspoon crushed red pepper
flakes

1. Cook sausage, onions, mushrooms, and garlic in skillet over
medium heat for 10 minutes. Drain. Transfer to crock pot. 2. Stir in
remaining ingredients. 3. Cover. Cook on low 8 to 9 hours.

Savory Pork Roast with Sauerkraut

Prep time: 10 minutes | Cook time: 3 to 6 hours |
Serves 6

1 (2-pound / 907-g) pork roast
1 clove garlic, minced
1 medium onion, sliced

1 pint sauerkraut, or more if
you wish
1 teaspoon caraway seed

1. If you have time, heat a nonstick skillet over medium-high heat.
Place the roast in the hot pan and brown on all sides. 2. Place
the roast, browned or not, in the crock pot. 3. Add remaining
ingredients in the order listed. 4. Cover and cook on high 3 hours,
or on low 4 to 6 hours, or until meat is tender but not dry.

Pork and Sauerdogs

Prep time: 5 minutes | Cook time: 4 to 11 hours |
Serves 12 to 15

1 (5-pound / 2.3-kg) pork roast
1 (32-ounce / 907-g) can

sauerkraut, undrained
1 package of 8 hot dogs

1. Place pork in crock pot. Spoon sauerkraut over pork. 2. Cover
and cook on low 9 to 11 hours, or on high 4 to 5 hours, or until
meat is tender but not dry. 3. Lift roast onto a platter and, using a
fork, separate the meat into small pieces. 4. Return pork to cooker
and stir into sauerkraut. 5. Cut hot dogs into ½-inch slices and stir
into pork and sauerkraut. 6. Cover and cook for an additional 30
minutes. Serve.

Hot Dogs and Noodles

Prep time: 25 minutes | Cook time: 5 to 6 hours |
Serves 6

1 (8-ounce / 227-g) package
medium egg noodles, cooked
and drained
1¼ cups grated Parmesan
cheese
1 cup milk
¼ cup butter or margarine,
melted

1 tablespoon flour
¼ teaspoon salt
1 (1-pound / 454-g) package
hot dogs, sliced
¼ cup packed brown sugar
¼ cup mayonnaise
2 tablespoons prepared mustard

1. Place noodles, cheese, milk, butter, flour, and salt in crock pot.
Mix well. 2. Combine hot dogs with remaining ingredients. Spoon
evenly over noodles. 3. Cover. Cook on low 5 to 6 hours.

Stuffed Green Peppers with Corn

Prep time: 20 minutes | Cook time: 5 to 6 hours | Serves 6

6 green bell peppers
½ pound (227 g) extra-lean ground beef
¼ cup finely chopped onions
1 tablespoon chopped pimento
¾ teaspoon salt
¼ teaspoon black pepper
1 (12-ounce / 340-g) can low-sodium whole-kernel corn, drained
1 tablespoon Worcestershire sauce
1 teaspoon prepared mustard
1 (10¾-ounce / 305-g) can condensed low-sodium cream of tomato soup

1. Cut a slice off the top of each pepper. 2. Remove core, seeds, and white membrane. In a small bowl, combine beef, onions, pimento, salt, black pepper, and corn. 3. Spoon into peppers. Stand peppers up in crock pot. 4. Combine Worcestershire sauce, mustard, and tomato soup. Pour over peppers. 5. Cover. Cook on low 5 to 6 hours.

Barbecued Hot Dogs

Prep time: 5 minutes | Cook time: 4½ hours | Serves 8

1 cup apricot preserves
4 ounces (113 g) tomato sauce
⅓ cup vinegar
2 tablespoons soy sauce
2 tablespoons honey
1 tablespoon oil
1 teaspoon salt
¼ teaspoon ground ginger
2 pounds (907 g) hot dogs, cut into 1-inch pieces

1. Combine all ingredients except hot dogs in crock pot. 2. Cover. Cook on high 30 minutes. Add hot dog pieces. Cook on low 4 hours. 3. Serve as an appetizer.

Easy Meatballs for a Group

Prep time: 5 minutes | Cook time: 4 hours | Serves 10 to 12

80 to 100 frozen small meatballs
1 (16-ounce / 454-g) jar barbecue sauce
1 (16-ounce / 454-g) jar apricot jam

1. Fill crock pot with meatballs. 2. Combine sauce and jam. Pour over meatballs. 3. Cover. Cook on low 4 hours, stirring occasionally. 4. Serve as an appetizer, or as a main dish.

Steak in a Crock

Prep time: 20 minutes | Cook time: 8 to 12 hours | Serves 4 to 5

1 medium onion, sliced and separated into rings
1 (4-ounce / 113-g) can of sliced mushrooms, liquid reserved
2 (2½-pound / 1.1-kg) round steak, ¾-inch thick, cut into 4 to 5 pieces
1 (10¾-ounce / 305-g) can cream of mushroom soup
2 tablespoons dry sherry or water

1. Put onion rings and mushrooms in bottom of crock pot. 2. Brown meat in nonstick skillet on all sides. Place in crock pot over top vegetables. 3. In a bowl, mix reserved mushroom liquid, soup, and sherry together. Pour over all. 4. Cover and cook on low 8 to 12 hours, or until meat is tender but not overcooked.

Roast Venison with Gravy

Prep time: 5 minutes | Cook time: 6 to 7 hours | Serves 4 to 6

1 (2- to 3-pound / 907-g to 1.4-kg) venison roast
1 to 2 teaspoons garlic powder or onion powder
1 (10¾-ounce / 305-g) can golden mushroom soup
¾ soup can of water

1. Place roast in crock pot. Sprinkle both sides with seasoning. 2. Cover and cook on low 4 to 5 hours, turning the roast twice while cooking. 3. In a bowl, mix together soup and water. Add to meat after it's cooked for 4 to 5 hours. 4. Cover and cook on low 2 more hours, turning roast once during this time.

Southwestern Flair

Prep time: 5 minutes | Cook time: 9 hours | Serves 8 to 12

1 (3- to 4-pound / 1.4- to 1.8-kg) chuck roast or flank steak
1 envelope dry taco seasoning
1 cup chopped onions
1 tablespoon white vinegar
1¼ cup green chilies
Flour tortillas

1. Combine meat, taco seasoning, onions, vinegar, and chilies in crock pot. 2. Cover. Cook on low 9 hours. 3. Shred meat with fork. 4. Serve with tortillas.

Stuffed "Baked" Topping

Prep time: 35 minutes | Cook time: 1 hour | Serves 12

3 pounds (1.4 kg) ground beef	¾ pound (340 g) Cheddar
1 cup chopped green peppers	cheese
½ cup chopped onions	¾ pound (340 g) your favorite
6 tablespoons butter	mild cheese
¼ cup flour	½ teaspoon hot pepper sauce
3 cups milk	¼ teaspoon dry mustard
½ cup pimento or chopped	Salt to taste
sweet red peppers	12 baked potatoes

1. Brown ground beef, green peppers, and onions in butter. Transfer mixture to crock pot, reserving drippings. 2. Stir flour into drippings. Slowly add milk. Cook until thickened. 3. Add pimento, cheeses, and seasonings. Pour over ingredients in crock pot. 4. Cover. Heat on low. 5. Serve over baked potatoes, each one split open on an individual dinner plate.

Fruity Corned Beef and Cabbage

Prep time: 10 minutes | Cook time: 5 to 12 hours | Serves 6

2 medium onions, sliced	2 teaspoons finely shredded
1 (2½- to 3-pound / 1.1- to 1.4-kg) corned beef brisket	orange peel
	6 whole cloves
1 cup apple juice	2 teaspoons prepared mustard
¼ cup brown sugar, packed	6 cabbage wedges

1. Place onions in crock pot. Place beef on top of onions. 2. Combine apple juice, brown sugar, orange peel, cloves, and mustard. Pour over meat. 3. Place cabbage on top. 4. Cover. Cook on low 10 to 12 hours, or on high 5 to 6 hours.

crock pot Chili

Prep time: 25 minutes | Cook time: 6 to 12 hours | Serves 8 to 10

3 pounds (1.4 kg) beef stewing meat, browned	1 to 1½ onions, chopped, according to your taste
2 cloves garlic, minced	preference
¼ teaspoon pepper	½ teaspoon salt
½ teaspoon cumin	½ teaspoon dried oregano
¼ teaspoon dry mustard	1 tablespoon chili powder
1 (7½-ounce / 213-g) can jalapeño relish	1 (7-ounce / 198-g) can green chilies, chopped
1 cup beef broth	1 (14½-ounce / 411-g) can

stewed tomatoes, chopped
1 (15-ounce / 425-g) can tomato sauce
2 (15-ounce / 425-g) cans

red kidney beans, rinsed and drained
2 (15-ounce / 425-g) cans pinto beans, rinsed and drained

1. Combine all ingredients except kidney and pinto beans in crock pot. 2. Cover. Cook on low 10 to 12 hours, or on high 6 to 7 hours. Add beans halfway through cooking time. 3. Serve.

Meat Loaf and Mexico

Prep time: 15 minutes | Cook time: 4 to 4½ hours | Serves 6

1¼ pounds (567 g) extra-lean ground beef	soup mix
	2 tablespoons low-sodium taco
4 cups hash browns, thawed	seasoning
1 egg, lightly beaten, or egg substitute	2 cups fat-free shredded Cheddar cheese, divided
2 tablespoons dry vegetable	Nonfat cooking spray

1. Mix together ground beef, hash browns, egg, soup mix, taco seasoning, and 1 cup of cheese. Shape into loaf. 2. Line crock pot with tin foil, allowing ends of foil to extend out over edges of cooker, enough to grab hold of and to lift the loaf out when it's finished cooking. Spray the foil with nonfat cooking spray. 3. Place loaf in cooker. Cover. Cook on low 4 hours. 4. Sprinkle with remaining cheese and cover until melted. 5. Gently lift loaf out, using foil handles. Allow to rest 10 minutes, then slice and serve.

Tiajuana Tacos

Prep time: 20 minutes | Cook time: 2 hours | Serves 6

3 cups cooked chopped beef	¼ teaspoon pepper
1 (1-pound / 454-g) can refried beans	¼ teaspoon paprika
	⅛ teaspoon celery salt
½ cup chopped onions	⅛ teaspoon ground nutmeg
½ cup chopped green peppers	¾ cup water
½ cup chopped ripe olives	1 teaspoon salt
1 (8-ounce / 227-g) can tomato sauce	1 cup crushed corn chips
	6 taco shells
3 teaspoons chili powder	Shredded lettuce
1 tablespoon Worcestershire sauce	Chopped tomatoes
	Shredded Cheddar cheese
½ teaspoon garlic powder	

1. Combine first 15 ingredients in crock pot. 2. Cover. Cook on high 2 hours. 3. Just before serving, fold in corn chips. 4. Spoon mixture into taco shells. Top with lettuce, tomatoes, and cheese.

Tender Pork Roast

Prep time: 10 minutes | Cook time: 3 to 8 hours | Serves 8

1 (3-pound / 1.4-kg) boneless pork roast, cut in half	¾ cup soy sauce
1 (8-ounce / 227-g) can tomato sauce	½ cup sugar
	2 teaspoons dry mustard

1. Place roast in crock pot. 2. Combine remaining ingredients in a bowl. Pour over roast. 3. Cover and cook on low 6 to 8 hours, or on high 3 to 4 hours, or until meat is tender but not dry. 4. Remove roast from crock pot to a serving platter. Discard juices or thicken for gravy.

A-Touch-of-Italy Meat Loaf

Prep time: 10 minutes | Cook time: 2½ to 6 hours | Serves 8

2 pounds (907 g) ground beef	¼ teaspoon pepper
2 cups soft bread crumbs	1¼ teaspoons salt
½ cup spaghetti sauce plus 2 tablespoons, divided	1 teaspoon garlic salt
1 large egg	½ teaspoon dried Italian herbs
2 tablespoons dried onion	¼ teaspoon garlic powder

1. Fold a 30-inch-long piece of foil in half lengthwise. Place in bottom of crock pot with both ends hanging over the edge of cooker. Grease foil. 2. Combine beef, bread crumbs, ½ cup spaghetti sauce, egg, onion, and seasonings. Shape into loaf. Place on top of foil in crock pot. Spread 2 tablespoons spaghetti sauce over top. 3. Cover. Cook on high 2½ to 3 hours, or on low 5 to 6 hours.

So-Easy Roast Beef

Prep time: 5 minutes | Cook time: 6 to 8 hours | Serves 6 to 8

1 (3- to 4-pound / 1.4- to 1.8-kg) beef roast	cream of mushroom soup
1 (10¾-ounce / 305-g) can	Half or all of 1 envelope dry onion soup mix

1. Rinse beef, pat dry, and place in crock pot. 2. Pour mushroom soup over top. Sprinkle with dry soup mix. 3. Cover and cook on low 6 to 8 hours, or until meat is tender but not dry.

Green Beans with Sausage

Prep time: 5 minutes | Cook time: 4 to 5 hours | Serves 4 to 5

1 (16-ounce / 454-g) package miniature smoked sausage links	1 small onion, chopped
1 quart green beans, with most of the juice drained	½ cup brown sugar
	¼ cup ketchup

1. Place sausage in crock pot. Top with beans and then onion. 2. In a bowl, stir together sugar and ketchup. Spoon over top. 3. Cover and cook on low 4 to 5 hours.

Sour Beef

Prep time: 5 minutes | Cook time: 8 to 10 hours | Serves 6 to 8

1 (3- to 4-pound / 1.4- to 1.8-kg) pot roast	3 bay leaves
⅓ cup cider vinegar	½ teaspoon salt
1 large onion, sliced	¼ teaspoon ground cloves
	¼ teaspoon garlic powder

1. Place roast in crock pot. Add remaining ingredients. 2. Cover. Cook on low 8 to 10 hours.

Our Favorite Chili

Prep time: 20 minutes | Cook time: 4 to 10 hours | Serves 10 to 12

1½ pounds (680 g) ground beef	2 teaspoons vinegar
¼ cup chopped onions	1½ teaspoons brown sugar
1 rib celery, chopped	1½ teaspoons salt
1 (29-ounce / 822-g) can stewed tomatoes	1 teaspoon Worcestershire sauce
2 (15½-ounce / 439-g) cans red kidney beans, undrained	½ teaspoon garlic powder
2 (16-ounce / 454-g) cans chili beans, undrained	½ teaspoon dry mustard powder
½ cup ketchup	1 tablespoon chili powder
1½ teaspoons lemon juice	2 (6-ounce / 170-g) cans tomato paste

1. Brown ground beef, onions, and celery in skillet. Drain. Place in crock pot. 2. Add remaining ingredients. Mix well. 3. Cover. Cook on low 8 to 10 hours, or on high 4 to 5 hours. 4. Serve.

Cheeseburger Casserole

Prep time: 20 minutes | Cook time: 3 hours | Serves 6

1 pound (454 g) ground beef	1 egg
1 small onion, chopped	Tomato juice to moisten
1 teaspoon salt	4½ cups mashed potatoes
Dash of pepper	9 slices American cheese
½ cup bread crumbs	

1. Combine beef, onions, salt, pepper, bread crumbs, egg, and tomato juice. Place one-third of mixture in crock pot. 2. Spread with one-third of mashed potatoes and 3 slices cheese. Repeat 2 times. 3. Cover. Cook on low 3 hours.

Pizza Rice Casserole

Prep time: 20 minutes | Cook time: 6 hours | Serves 6 to 8

1 pound (454 g) ground beef	3 cups shredded cheese, your
1 medium onion, chopped	choice of flavor
3 cups long-grain rice,	1 cup cottage cheese (optional)
uncooked	4 cups water
1 quart pizza sauce	

1. Place ground beef and chopped onion in a nonstick skillet. Brown and then drain. 2. Mix all ingredients in crock pot. 3. Cover and cook on high for 6 hours, or until the rice is tender.

Meat Loaf and Mushrooms

Prep time: 20 minutes | Cook time: 5 hours | Serves 6

2 (1-ounce / 28-g) slices whole wheat bread	1 teaspoon Italian seasoning
½ pound (227 g) extra-lean ground beef	¾ teaspoon salt
	2 eggs
¾ pound (340 g) fat-free ground turkey	1 clove garlic, minced
	3 tablespoons ketchup
1½ cups mushrooms, sliced	1½ teaspoons Dijon mustard
½ cup minced onions	⅛ teaspoon ground red pepper

1. Fold two strips of tin foil, each long enough to fit from the top of the cooker, down inside and up the other side, plus a 2-inch overhang on each side of the cooker—to function as handles for lifting the finished loaf out of the cooker. 2. Process bread slices in food processor until crumbs measure 1⅓ cups. 3. Combine bread crumbs, beef, turkey, mushrooms, onions, Italian seasoning, salt, eggs, and garlic in bowl. Shape into loaf to fit in crock pot. 4. Mix together ketchup, mustard, and pepper. Spread over top of loaf. 5. Cover. Cook on low 5 hours. 6. When finished, pull loaf up gently with foil handles. Place loaf on warm platter. Pull foil handles away. Allow loaf to rest for 10 minutes before slicing.

Shredded Beef for Tacos

Prep time: 15 minutes | Cook time: 6 to 8 hours | Serves 6 to 8

1 (2- to 3-pound / 907-g to 1.4-kg) round roast, cut into large chunks	2 serrano chilies, chopped
	3 garlic cloves, minced
	1 teaspoon salt
1 large onion, chopped	1 cup water
3 tablespoons oil	

1. Brown meat and onion in oil. Transfer to crock pot. 2. Add chilies, garlic, salt, and water. 3. Cover. Cook on high 6 to 8 hours. 4. Pull meat apart with two forks until shredded. 5. Serve.

Black Beans with Ham

Prep time: 20 minutes | Cook time: 10 to 12 hours | Serves 8 to 10

4 cups dry black beans	2 garlic cloves, minced
1 to 2 cups diced ham	3 bay leaves
1 teaspoon salt (optional)	1 quart diced tomatoes
1 teaspoon cumin	1 tablespoon brown sugar
½ to 1 cup minced onion	

1. Cover black beans with water and soak for 8 hours, or overnight. Drain and pour beans into crock pot. 2. Add all remaining ingredients and stir well. Cover with water. 3. Cover cooker. Cook on low 10 to 12 hours. 4. Serve.

Nutritious Meat Loaf

Prep time: 10 minutes | Cook time: 3 to 4 hours | Serves 6

1 pound (454 g) ground beef	1 tablespoon dried onion flakes
2 cups finely shredded cabbage	½ teaspoon caraway seeds
1 medium green pepper, diced	1 teaspoon salt

1. Combine all ingredients. Shape into loaf and place on rack in crock pot. 2. Cover. Cook on high 3 to 4 hours.

No-Fuss Sauerkraut

Prep time: 7 minutes | Cook time: 4 to 5 hours |
Serves 12

1 (3-pound / 1.4-kg) pork roast
3 (2-pound / 907-g) packages sauerkraut (drain and discard juice from 1 package)

2 apples, peeled and sliced
½ cup brown sugar
1 cup apple juice

1. Place meat in large crock pot. 2. Place sauerkraut on top of meat. 3. Add apples and brown sugar. Add apple juice. 4. Cover. Cook on high 4 to 5 hours. 5. Serve.

1-2 to 3-4 Casserole

Prep time: 35 minutes | Cook time: 7 to 9 hours |
Serves 8

1 pound (454 g) ground beef
2 onions, sliced
3 carrots, thinly sliced
4 potatoes, thinly sliced
½ teaspoon salt
⅛ teaspoon pepper
1 cup cold water

½ teaspoon cream of tartar
1 (10¾-ounce / 305-g) can cream of mushroom soup
¼ cup milk
½ teaspoon salt
⅛ teaspoon pepper

1. Layer in greased crock pot: ground beef, onions, carrots, ½ teaspoon salt, and ⅛ teaspoon pepper. 2. Dissolve cream of tartar in water in bowl. Toss sliced potatoes with water. 3. Drain. Combine soup and milk. Toss with potatoes. Add remaining salt and pepper. Arrange potatoes in crock pot. 4. Cover. Cook on low 7 to 9 hours.

Spanish Rice

Prep time: 15 minutes | Cook time: 6 to 10 hours |
Serves 8

2 pounds (907 g) ground beef, browned
2 medium onions, chopped
2 green peppers, chopped
1 (28-ounce / 794-g) can tomatoes
1 (8-ounce / 227-g) can tomato

sauce
1½ cups water
2½ teaspoons chili powder
2 teaspoons salt
2 teaspoons Worcestershire sauce
1½ cups rice, uncooked

1. Combine all ingredients in crock pot. 2. Cover. Cook on low 8 to 10 hours, or on high 6 hours.

Taters 'n Beef

Prep time: 20 minutes | Cook time: 4¼ to 6¼ hours |
Serves 6 to 8

2 pounds (907 g) ground beef, browned
1 teaspoon salt
½ teaspoon pepper

¼ cup chopped onions
1 cup canned tomato soup
6 potatoes, sliced
1 cup milk

1. Combined beef, salt, pepper, onions, and soup. 2. Place a layer of potatoes in bottom of crock pot. Cover with a portion of the meat mixture. Repeat layers until ingredients are used. 3. Cover. Cook on low 4 to 6 hours. Add milk and cook on high 15 to 20 minutes.

Surprise Stuffed Peppers

Prep time: 15 minutes | Cook time: 8 to 9 hours |
Serves 4

2 cups low-sodium tomato juice
1 (6-ounce / 170-g) can tomato paste
2 (7-ounce / 198-g) cans chunk-style tuna, drained and rinsed
2 tablespoons dried onion flakes

2 tablespoons dried veggie flakes
¼ teaspoon garlic powder
4 medium green bell peppers, tops removed and seeded

1. Mix tomato juice and tomato paste, reserving 1 cup. 2. Mix remaining tomato-juice mixture with tuna, onion flakes, veggie flakes, and garlic powder. 3. Fill peppers equally with mixture. Place upright in crock pot. 4. Pour the reserved 1 cup tomato-juice mixture over peppers. 5. Cover. Cook on low 8 to 9 hours, or until peppers are done to your liking.

Beef and Pepper Rice

Prep time: 20 minutes | Cook time: 3 to 6 hours |
Serves 4 to 6

1 pound (454 g) ground beef
2 green peppers, or 1 green and 1 red pepper, coarsely chopped
1 cup chopped onions

1 cup brown rice, uncooked
2 beef bouillon cubes, crushed
3 cups water
1 tablespoon soy sauce

1. Brown beef in skillet. Drain. 2. Combine all ingredients in crock pot. Mix well. 3. Cover. Cook on low 5 to 6 hours or on high 3 hours, or until liquid is absorbed.

Beef Pot Roast

Prep time: 10 minutes | Cook time: 6 to 7 hours |
Serves 6 to 8

1 (4- to 5-pound / 1.8- to 2.3-kg) beef chuck roast
1 garlic clove, cut in half
Salt to taste
Pepper to taste
1 carrot, chopped

1 rib celery, chopped
1 small onion, sliced
¾ cup sour cream
3 tablespoons flour
½ cup dry white wine

1. Rub roast with garlic. Season with salt and pepper. Place in crock pot. 2. Add carrots, celery, and onion. 3. Combine sour cream, flour, and wine. Pour into crock pot. 4. Cover. Cook on low 6 to 7 hours.

Chili Hot Dogs

Prep time: 10 minutes | Cook time: 2 to 3 hours |
Serves 4 to 5

1 package hot dogs, cut into ¾-inch slices
1 (28-ounce / 794-g) can baked beans

1 teaspoon prepared mustard
1 teaspoon instant minced onion
⅓ cup chili sauce

1. In crock pot, combine all ingredients. 2. Cover and cook on low 2 to 3 hours. 3. Serve.

Spanish Round Steak

Prep time: 10 minutes | Cook time: 8 hours | Serves
4 to 6

1 small onion, sliced, divided
1 rib celery, chopped, divided
1 green bell pepper, sliced in rings, divided
2 pounds (907 g) round steak
2 tablespoons chopped fresh parsley, or 2 teaspoons dried parsley

1 tablespoon Worcestershire sauce
1 tablespoon dry mustard
1 tablespoon chili powder
2 cups canned tomatoes
2 teaspoons dry minced garlic
½ teaspoon salt
¼ teaspoon pepper

1. Put half of onion, celery, and green pepper, in crock pot. 2. Cut steak into serving-size pieces. Place steak pieces in crock pot. 3. Put remaining onion, celery, and green pepper over steak. 4. Combine remaining ingredients. Pour over meat. 5. Cover. Cook on low 8 hours. 6. Serve.

Cabbage and Corned Beef

Prep time: 15 minutes | Cook time: 5 to 10 hours |
Serves 12

3 large carrots, cut into chunks
1 cup chopped celery
1 teaspoon salt
½ teaspoon black pepper
1 cup water
1 (4-pound / 1.8-kg) corned

beef
1 large onion, cut into pieces
4 potatoes, peeled and chunked
Half a small head of cabbage, cut in wedges

1. Place carrots, celery, seasonings, and water in crock pot. 2. Add beef. Cover with onions. 3. Cover. Cook on low 8 to 10 hours, or on high 5 to 6 hours. (If your schedule allows, this dish has especially good taste and texture if you begin it on high for 1 hour, and then turn it to low for 5 to 6 hours, before going on to Step 4.) 4. Lift corned beef out of cooker and add potatoes, pushing them to bottom of crock pot. Return beef to cooker. 5. Cover. Cook on low 1 hour. 6. Lift corned beef out of cooker and add cabbage, pushing the wedges down into the broth. Return beef to cooker. 7. Cover. Cook on low 1 more hour. 8. Remove corned beef. Cool and slice on the diagonal. Serve surrounded by vegetables.

Autumn Harvest Pork Loin

Prep time: 30 minutes | Cook time: 5 to 6 hours |
Serves 4 to 6

1 cup cider or apple juice
1 (1½- to 2-pound / 680- to 907-g) pork loin
Salt
Pepper
2 large Granny Smith apples, peeled and sliced

1½ whole butternut squashes, peeled and cubed
½ cup brown sugar
¼ teaspoon cinnamon
¼ teaspoon dried thyme
¼ teaspoon dried sage

1. Heat cider in hot skillet. Sear pork loin on all sides in cider. 2. Sprinkle meat with salt and pepper on all sides. Place in crock pot, along with juices. 3. Combine apples and squash. Sprinkle with sugar and herbs. Stir. Place around pork loin. 4. Cover. Cook on low 5 to 6 hours. 5. Remove pork from cooker. Let stand 10 to 15 minutes. Slice into ½-inch-thick slices. 6. Serve topped with apples and squash.

Seasoned Pork Ribs

Prep time: 10 minutes | Cook time: 4 hours | Serves 2 to 3

3 pounds (1.4 kg) pork shoulder ribs, cut in serving-size pieces	(optional) 1 tablespoon prepared
2 teaspoons chipotle seasoning spice	horseradish ¼ cup ketchup
1 teaspoon coarse black pepper	¼ cup apricot jelly

1. Heat a nonstick skillet over medium-high heat. 2. Season pork with chipotle seasonings and then place in hot skillet, browning each piece on top and bottom. Do in batches so all the pieces brown well. 3. As you finish browning ribs, place them in the crock pot. 4. Cover and cook on high for 3 hours. 5. Meanwhile, mix together pepper if you wish, horseradish, ketchup, and apricot jelly in a bowl. Spread over cooked pork. 6. Cover and cook on high 1 hour, or until the meat is tender.

Creamy Easy Meatballs

Prep time: 7 minutes | Cook time: 4 to 5 hours | Serves 10 to 12

2 (10¾-ounce / 305-g) cans cream of mushroom soup	mushrooms, undrained 1 cup milk
2 (8-ounce / 227-g) packages cream cheese, softened	2 to 3 pounds (907 g to 1.4 kg) frozen meatballs
1 (4-ounce / 113-g) can sliced	

1. Combine soup, cream cheese, mushrooms, and milk in crock pot. 2. Add meatballs. Stir. 3. Cover. Cook on low 4 to 5 hours. 4. Serve over noodles.

Veal and Peppers

Prep time: 10 minutes | Cook time: 4 to 7 hours | Serves 4

1½ pounds (680 g) boneless veal, cubed	1 teaspoon salt ½ teaspoon dried basil
3 green peppers, quartered	2 cloves garlic, minced
2 onions, thinly sliced	1 (28-ounce / 794-g) can
½ pound (227 g) fresh mushrooms, sliced	tomatoes

1. Combine all ingredients in crock pot. 2. Cover. Cook on low 7 hours, or on high 4 hours. 3. Serve.

Dilled Pot Roast

Prep time: 5 minutes | Cook time: 7¼ to 9¼ hours | Serves 8

1 (2¾-pound / 1.3-kg) beef pot roast	¼ cup water 2 tablespoons wine vinegar
1 teaspoon salt	4 tablespoons flour
¼ teaspoon black pepper	½ cup water
2 teaspoons dried dill weed, divided	2 cups fat-free sour cream

1. Sprinkle both sides of beef with salt, pepper, and 1 teaspoon dill weed. Place in crock pot. 2. Add ¼ cup water and vinegar. 3. Cover. Cook on low 7 to 9 hours. 4. Remove meat from pot. Turn cooker to high. 5. Stir flour into ½ cup water. Stir into meat drippings. 6. Stir in additional 1 teaspoon dill weed if you wish. 7. Cover. Cook on high 5 minutes. 8. Stir in sour cream. 9. Cover. Cook on high another 5 minutes. 10. Slice beef and serve.

Sesame Pork Ribs

Prep time: 20 minutes | Cook time: 5 to 6 hours | Serves 6

1 medium onion, sliced	¼ to ½ teaspoon crushed red
¾ cup packed brown sugar	pepper flakes
¼ cup soy sauce	5 pounds (2.3 kg) country-style
½ cup ketchup	pork ribs
¼ cup honey	2 tablespoons sesame seeds,
2 tablespoons cider or white vinegar	toasted 2 tablespoons chopped green
3 garlic cloves, minced	onions
1 teaspoon ground ginger	

1. Place onions in bottom of crock pot. 2. Combine brown sugar, soy sauce, ketchup, honey, vinegar, garlic, ginger, and red pepper flakes in large bowl. Add ribs and turn to coat. Place on top of onions in crock pot. Pour sauce over meat. 3. Cover. Cook on low 5 to 6 hours. 4. Place ribs on serving platter. Sprinkle with sesame seeds and green onions. Serve sauce on the side.

Chapter 5 Snacks and Appetizers

Chili Rellanos

Prep time: 15 minutes | Cook time: 6 to 8 hours | Serves 8

1¼ cups milk
4 eggs, beaten
3 tablespoons flour
1 (12-ounce / 340-g) can

chopped green chilies
2 cups shredded Cheddar cheese

1. Combine all ingredients in crock pot until well blended. 2. Cover and cook on low for 6 to 8 hours. 3. Serve.

Curried Almonds

Prep time: 5 minutes | Cook time: 3 to 4½ hours | Makes 4 cups nuts

2 tablespoons butter, melted
1 tablespoon curry powder
½ teaspoon seasoned salt

1 pound (454 g) blanched almonds

1. Combine butter with curry powder and seasoned salt. 2. Pour over almonds in crock pot. Mix to coat well. 3. Cover. Cook on low 2 to 3 hours. Turn to high. Uncover cooker and cook 1 to 1½ hours. 4. Serve hot or cold.

Slow Cooked Smokies

Prep time: 5 minutes | Cook time: 6 to 7 hours | Serves 12 to 16

2 pounds (907 g) miniature smoked sausage links
1 (28-ounce / 794-g) bottle barbecue sauce
1¼ cups water

3 tablespoons Worcestershire sauce
3 tablespoons steak sauce
½ teaspoon pepper

1. In a crock pot, combine all ingredients. Mix well. 2. Cover and cook on low 6 to 7 hours.

Sweet 'n' Spicy Crunchy Snack Mix

Prep time: 5 minutes | Cook time: 1½ hours | Makes 5½ cups

1 cup raw cashews
1 cup raw almonds
1 cup raw pecan halves
1 cup walnuts
½ cup raw pepitas
½ cup raw sunflower seeds

¼ cup aquafaba
¼ cup maple syrup (optional)
1 teaspoon miso paste
1 teaspoon garlic powder
1 teaspoon paprika
2 teaspoons ground ginger

1. Put the cashews, almonds, pecans, walnuts, pepitas, and sunflower seeds in the crock pot. 2. In a deep bowl, whisk or use an immersion blender to beat the aquafaba until foamy, about 1 minute. Add the maple syrup (if using), miso paste, garlic powder, paprika, and ginger and whisk or blend to combine. Pour over the nuts in the crock pot and gently toss, making sure all the nuts and seeds are coated. 3. Stretch a clean dish towel or several layers of paper towels over the top of the crock pot, but not touching the food, and place the lid on top. Cook on Low for 1½ hours, stirring every 20 to 30 minutes to keep the nuts from burning. After each stir, dry any condensation under the lid and replace the towels before re-covering. 4. Line a rimmed baking sheet with parchment paper. Transfer the snack mix to the baking sheet to cool. Store in an airtight container for up to 2 weeks.

Tangy Meatballs

Prep time: 15 minutes | Cook time: 2 to 4 hours | Makes 50 to 60 meatballs

2 pounds (907 g) precooked meatballs
1 (16-ounce / 454-g) bottle

barbecue sauce
8 ounces (227 g) grape jelly

1. Place meatballs in crock pot. 2. Combine barbecue sauce and jelly in medium-sized mixing bowl. 3. Pour over meatballs and stir well. 4. Cover and cook on high 2 hours, or on low 4 hours. 5. Turn to low and serve.

Barbecued Lil' Smokies

Prep time: 5 minutes | Cook time: 4 hours | Serves 48 to 60 as an appetizer

4 (16-ounce / 454-g) packages little smokies
1 (18-ounce / 510-g) bottle barbecue sauce

1. Mix ingredients together in crock pot. 2. Cover and cook on low for 4 hours.

All American Snack

Prep time: 10 minutes | Cook time: 3 hours | Makes 3 quarts snack mix

3 cups thin pretzel sticks	1 teaspoon garlic powder
4 cups Wheat Chex	1 teaspoon celery salt
4 cups Cheerios	½ teaspoon seasoned salt
1 (12-ounce / 340-g) can salted peanuts	2 tablespoons grated Parmesan cheese
¼ cup butter, melted	

1. Combine pretzels, cereal, and peanuts in large bowl. 2. Melt butter. Stir in garlic powder, celery salt, seasoned salt, and Parmesan cheese. Pour over pretzels and cereal. Toss until well mixed. 3. Pour into large crock pot. Cover. Cook on low 2½ hours, stirring every 30 minutes. Remove lid and cook another 30 minutes on low. 4. Serve warm or at room temperature. Store in tightly covered container.

Cheesy Tomato Pizza Fondue

Prep time: 15 minutes | Cook time: 1 hour | Serves 4 to 6

1 (1-pound / 454-g) block of cheese, your choice of good melting cheese, cut in ½-inch cubes
2 cups shredded Mozzarella cheese
1 (19-ounce / 539-g) can Italian-style stewed tomatoes with juice
Loaf of Italian bread, slices toasted and then cut into 1-inch cubes

1. Place cheese cubes, shredded Mozzarella cheese, and tomatoes in a lightly greased crock pot. 2. Cover and cook on high 45 to 60 minutes, or until cheese is melted. 3. Stir occasionally and scrape down sides of crock pot with rubber spatula to prevent scorching. 4. Reduce heat to low and serve. (Fondue will keep a smooth consistency for up to 4 hours.) 5. Serve with toasted bread cubes for dipping.

White Bean Tzatziki Dip

Prep time: 10 minutes | Cook time: 1 to 2 hours | Makes about 8 cups

4 (14½-ounce / 411-g) cans white beans, drained and rinsed	needed
8 garlic cloves, minced	Juice from one lemon, divided
1 medium onion, coarsely chopped	2 teaspoons dried dill, divided
¼ cup store-bought low-sodium vegetable broth, plus more as	Salt (optional)
	1 cucumber, peeled and finely diced

1. Place the beans, garlic, onion, broth, and half the lemon juice in a blender. Blend until creamy, about 1 minute, adding up to ¼ cup of additional broth as needed to make the mixture creamy. 2. Transfer the mixture to the crock pot, stir in 1 teaspoon of dill, and season with salt (if using). Cover and cook on Low for 1 to 2 hours until heated through. 3. Meanwhile, in a medium bowl, mix the cucumber with the remaining 1 teaspoon of dill and the remaining half of the lemon juice. Toss to coat. Season with salt (if using). 4. Spoon the dip from the crock pot into a serving bowl and top with the cucumber mixture before serving.

Eggplant Caponata Bruschetta

Prep time: 20 minutes | Cook time: 2 to 3 hours | Serves 4 to 8

1 medium eggplant, unpeeled and chopped	1 tablespoon maple syrup (optional)
1 medium onion, diced	1 teaspoon dried basil
2 small zucchini, diced	1 teaspoon dried oregano
3 celery stalks, diced	Ground black pepper
4 garlic cloves, minced	Salt (optional)
1 cup sliced pitted green olives	1 long thin loaf crusty whole-grain bread
2 (14½-ounce / 411-g) cans diced tomatoes	3 tablespoons chopped fresh flat-leaf parsley
2 tablespoons capers, drained	
¼ cup red wine vinegar	

1. Put the eggplant, onion, zucchini, celery, garlic, and olives in the crock pot. Pour in the tomatoes. Add the capers, vinegar, maple syrup (if using), basil, oregano, pepper, and salt (if using). Stir well to combine. Cover and cook on High for 2 to 3 hours or on Low for 5 to 6 hours. 2. Preheat the oven to 375°F (190°C). Slice the bread into ½-inch slices and place them on a baking sheet. Toast in the oven, keeping an eye on the bread so it doesn't burn. Flip the bread and toast the other side to make it into crostini. 3. After the caponata finishes cooking, stir in the parsley. Spoon about 2 tablespoons of caponata onto each piece of crostini and serve immediately.

Simmered Smoked Sausages

Prep time: 15 minutes | Cook time: 4 hours | Serves 16 to 20

2 (16-ounce / 454-g) packages miniature smoked sausage links
1 cup brown sugar, packed

½ cup ketchup
¼ cup prepared horseradish

1. Place sausages in crock pot. 2. Combine remaining ingredients in a bowl and pour over sausages. 3. Cover and cook on low for 4 hours.

Liver Paté

Prep time: 15 minutes | Cook time: 4 to 5 hours | Makes 1½ cups paté

1 pound (454 g) chicken livers
½ cup dry wine
1 teaspoon instant chicken bouillon
1 teaspoon minced parsley
1 tablespoon instant minced onion

¼ teaspoon ground ginger
½ teaspoon seasoned salt
1 tablespoon soy sauce
¼ teaspoon dry mustard
¼ cup soft butter
1 tablespoon brandy

1. In crock pot, combine all ingredients except butter and brandy. 2. Cover. Cook on low 4 to 5 hours. Let stand in liquid until cool. 3. Drain. Place in blender or food grinder. Add butter and brandy. Process until smooth. 4. Serve.

Cider Cheese Fondue—for a Buffet Table

Prep time: 15 minutes | Cook time: 4 minutes | Serves 4

¾ cup apple juice or cider
2 cups shredded Cheddar cheese
1 cup shredded Swiss cheese

1 tablespoon cornstarch
⅛ teaspoon pepper
1 pound (454 g) loaf French bread, cut into chunks

1. In a large saucepan, bring cider to a boil. Reduce heat to medium low. 2. In a large mixing bowl, toss together the cheeses with cornstarch and pepper. 3. Stir mixture into cider. Cook and stir for 3 to 4 minutes, or until cheese is melted. 4. Transfer to a 1-quart crock pot to keep warm. Stir occasionally 5. Serve with bread cubes for dipping.

Sausages in Wine

Prep time: 15 minutes | Cook time: 1 hour | Serves 6

1 cup dry red wine
2 tablespoons currant jelly

6 to 8 mild Italian sausages or Polish sausages

1. Place wine and jelly in crock pot. Heat until jelly is dissolved and sauce begins to simmer. Add sausages. 2. Cover and cook on high 45 minutes to 1 hour, or until sausages are cooked through and lightly glazed. 3. Transfer sausages to a cutting board and slice. Serve.

Mini Hot Dogs and Meatballs

Prep time: 5 minutes | Cook time: 2 to 3 hours | Serves 15

36 frozen cooked Italian meatballs (½-ounce / 14-g each)
1 (16-ounce / 454-g) package miniature hot dogs or little smoked sausages
1 (26-ounce / 737-g) jar

meatless spaghetti sauce
1 (18-ounce / 510-g) bottle barbecue sauce
1 (12-ounce / 340-g) bottle chili sauce

1. Combine all ingredients in crock pot. 2. Cover and cook on high 2 hours, or on low 3 hours, until heated through.

crock pot Candy

Prep time: 10 minutes | Cook time: 2 hours | Makes 80 to 100 pieces

1½ pounds (680 g) almond bark, broken
1 (4-ounce / 113-g) Baker's Brand German sweet chocolate bar, broken
8 ounces (227 g) chocolate

chips
8 ounces (227 g) peanut butter chips
2 pounds (907 g) lightly salted or unsalted peanuts

1. Spray inside of cooker with nonstick cooking spray. 2. Layer ingredients into crock pot in the order given above. 3. Cook on low 2 hours. Do not stir or lift the lid during the cooking time. 4. After 2 hours, mix well. 5. Drop by teaspoonfuls onto waxed paper. Refrigerate for approximately 45 minutes before serving or storing.

Sweet 'n Sour Meatballs

Prep time: 10 minutes | Cook time: 2 to 4 hours |
Serves 15 to 20

1 (12-ounce / 340-g) jar grape jelly	2 (1-pound / 454-g) bags prepared frozen meatballs, thawed
1 (12-ounce / 340-g) jar chili sauce	

1. Combine jelly and sauce in crock pot. Stir well. 2. Add meatballs. Stir to coat. 3. Cover and heat on low 4 hours, or on high 2 hours. Keep crock pot on low while serving.

Rosemary-Onion Jam

Prep time: 5 minutes | Cook time: 6 to 7 hours |
Makes 3 to 4 cups

4 to 6 large sweet onions (about 3 pounds / 1.4 kg), sliced into half-moons	¼ cup balsamic vinegar
2 garlic cloves, minced	1 teaspoon finely chopped fresh rosemary (about 2 sprigs), or dried
½ cup maple syrup (optional)	

1. Put the onions in the crock pot. Add the garlic. 2. In a small bowl, stir together the maple syrup (if using), vinegar, and rosemary. Pour the mixture into the crock pot and toss gently to coat the onions. Cover and cook on High for 6 to 7 hours or on Low for 10 to 12 hours, until the onions are deep brown. 3. Transfer the mixture to a blender, or use an immersion blender, and blend into a chunky jam consistency. Store in glass jars or plastic containers in the refrigerator for up to 1 month.

"Baked" Brie with Cranberry Chutney

Prep time: 10 minutes | Cook time: 4 hours | Serves
8 to 10

1 cup fresh or dried cranberries	⅛ teaspoon ground cloves
½ cup brown sugar	Oil
⅓ cup cider vinegar	1 (8-ounce / 227-g) round of Brie cheese
2 tablespoons water or orange juice	1 tablespoon sliced almonds, toasted
2 teaspoons minced crystallized ginger	Crackers
¼ teaspoon cinnamon	

1. Mix together cranberries, brown sugar, vinegar, water or juice, ginger, cinnamon, and cloves in crock pot. 2. Cover. Cook on low

4 hours. Stir once near the end to see if it is thickening. If not, remove lid, turn heat to high and cook 30 minutes without lid. 3. Put cranberry chutney in covered container and chill for up to 2 weeks. When ready to serve, bring to room temperature. 4. Brush ovenproof plate with oil, place unpeeled Brie on plate, and bake uncovered at 350ºF (180ºC) for 9 minutes, until cheese is soft and partially melted. Remove from oven. 5. Top with at least half the chutney and garnish with almonds. Serve with crackers.

Party Time Artichokes

Prep time: 10 minutes | Cook time: 2½ to 4 hours |
Serves 4

4 whole, fresh artichokes	divided
1 teaspoon salt	2 tablespoons butter, melted
4 tablespoons lemon juice,	

1. Wash and trim off the tough outer leaves and around the bottom of the artichokes. Cut off about 1 inch from the tops of each, and trim off the tips of the leaves. Spread the top leaves apart and use a long-handled spoon to pull out the fuzzy chokes in their centers. 2. Stand the prepared artichokes upright in the crock pot. Sprinkle each with ¼ teaspoon salt. 3. Spoon 2 tablespoons lemon juice over the artichokes. Pour in enough water to cover the bottom half of the artichokes. 4. Cover and cook on high for 2½ to 4 hours. 5. Serve with melted butter and remaining lemon juice for dipping.

Pineapple, Peach, and Mango Salsa

Prep time: 15 minutes | Cook time: 2 to 3 hours |
Makes about 6 cups

1 medium onion, finely diced	1 (15-ounce / 425-g) can no-sugar-added sliced peaches in juice, drained and finely diced
2 garlic cloves, minced	
1 medium orange, red, or yellow bell pepper, finely diced	½ teaspoon ground cumin
1 (20-ounce / 567-g) can crushed pineapple in juice	1 teaspoon paprika
	Juice of 1 lime
1 (15-ounce / 425-g) can no-sugar-added mango in juice, drained and finely diced	3 to 4 tablespoons chopped fresh mint (about 10 to 15 leaves)

1. Put the onion, garlic, and bell pepper in the crock pot. Add the pineapple and its juices, the mango, and the peaches. Sprinkle the cumin and paprika into the crock pot. Add the lime juice and stir well to combine. 2. Cover and cook on Low for 2 to 3 hours, or until the onion and peppers are cooked through and softened. Let the salsa cool slightly, then stir in the mint just before serving.

Crispy Chickpea Snackers

Prep time: 10 minutes | Cook time: 4 to 6 hours |
Makes 7 to 8 cups

4 (14½-ounce / 411-g) cans chickpeas, drained and rinsed	1 tablespoon onion powder
Juice of 2 lemons	2 teaspoons paprika
1 tablespoon garlic powder	Salt (optional)

1. Put the chickpeas into the crock pot. Add the lemon juice, garlic powder, onion powder, and paprika. Season with salt (if using). Toss gently to thoroughly coat every chickpea with the seasoning. 2. Cover the crock pot and, using a wooden spoon or a chopstick, prop open the lid to allow the steam to escape. Cook on High for 4 to 6 hours or on Low for 8 to 10 hours, stirring every 30 to 45 minutes to keep the chickpeas from burning.

Spinach and Artichoke Dip

Prep time: 20 minutes | Cook time: 5 hours | Serves 10

1 (15-ounce / 425-g) BPA-free can no-salt-added cannellini beans, drained and rinsed	1 (10-ounce / 283-g) bag chopped frozen spinach, thawed and drained
1 red onion, chopped	½ cup sour cream
3 garlic cloves, minced	2 tablespoons freshly squeezed
2 (14-ounce / 397-g) BPA-free cans no-salt-added artichoke hearts, drained and quartered	lemon juice
	2 tablespoons olive oil
	1 cup shredded Swiss cheese

1. In a 6-quart crock pot, mash the beans using a potato masher. 2. Stir in the onion, garlic, and artichoke hearts. 3. Stir in the spinach, sour cream, lemon juice, olive oil, and Swiss cheese. 4. Cover and cook on low for 4 to 5 hours, or until the dip is hot and bubbling.

Spiced Glazed Carrots

Prep time: 10 minutes | Cook time: 2 to 3 hours |
Serves 4 to 6

2 pounds (907 g) fresh baby carrots or frozen cut carrots	(optional)
⅓ cup no-sugar-added apricot preserves, such as Polaner All Fruit brand	¼ teaspoon ground cinnamon
	¼ teaspoon ground nutmeg
	¼ teaspoon ground turmeric
2 tablespoons orange juice	½ teaspoon ground ginger
1 tablespoon balsamic vinegar	1 teaspoon dried thyme
1 tablespoon maple syrup	1 tablespoon cornstarch
	2 tablespoons water

1. Place the carrots into the crock pot. In a measuring cup or medium bowl, stir together the apricot preserves, orange juice, vinegar, maple syrup (if using), cinnamon, nutmeg, turmeric, ginger, and thyme. Pour the sauce into the crock pot and stir to coat the carrots. Cover and cook on High for 2 to 3 hours or on Low for 4 to 6 hours. 2. During the last 30 minutes of cooking, add the cornstarch and water to a small lidded jar. Cover and shake the jar well to form a slurry and pour it into the crock pot, stirring occasionally to thicken the sauce and form a glaze.

Classic Italian Mushrooms

Prep time: 10 minutes | Cook time: 2 hours | Serves
4 to 6

2 pounds (907 g) white button mushrooms, stemmed	3 to 5 tablespoons store-bought low-sodium vegetable broth
4 garlic cloves, minced	3 teaspoons Italian seasoning
1 medium onion, sliced into half-moons	Ground black pepper
	Salt (optional)

1. Cut any extra-large mushrooms in half. Place the mushrooms in the crock pot. Add the garlic and onion. 2. Pour in the broth and sprinkle with the Italian seasoning. Season with black pepper and salt (if using). Stir to combine. Cover and cook on Low for 2 hours, or until the mushrooms are cooked through.

Tex-Mex Nacho Dip

Prep time: 20 minutes | Cook time: 8 hours | Serves 12

4 (5-ounce / 142-g) boneless, skinless chicken breasts	1 (15-ounce / 425-g) BPA-free can no-salt-added black beans, drained and rinsed
3 onions, chopped	
6 garlic cloves, minced	1 cup plain Greek yogurt
2 jalapeño peppers, minced	1 cup shredded Monterey Jack cheese
½ cup chicken stock	
2 tablespoons chili powder	2 avocados, peeled and chopped

1. In a 6-quart crock pot, mix the chicken, onions, garlic, and jalapeño peppers. Add the chicken stock and chili powder. Cover and cook on low for 5 to 7 hours, or until the chicken registers 165°F (74°C) on a food thermometer. 2. Remove the chicken from the crock pot and shred it using two forks. Return the chicken to the crock pot. 3. Add the black beans, yogurt, and cheese. Cover and cook on low 1 hour longer, until hot. 4. Top with the avocados and serve.

Spiced Chocolate-Nut Clusters

Prep time: 20 minutes | Cook time: 2 hours | Makes
60 candies

4 pounds (1.8 kg) dairy-free 70% to 80% cacao dark chocolate, chopped
¼ cup coconut oil
2 teaspoons vanilla extract

1 teaspoon ground cinnamon
¼ teaspoon ground cloves
4 cups roasted cashews
3 cups coarsely chopped pecans

1. In a 6-quart crock pot, mix the chopped chocolate, coconut oil, vanilla, cinnamon, and cloves. Cover and cook on low for 2 hours, or until the chocolate melts. 2. Stir the chocolate mixture until it is smooth. 3. Stir in the cashews and pecans. 4. Drop the mixture by tablespoons onto waxed paper or parchment paper. Let stand until set.

Mole Chicken Bites

Prep time: 20 minutes | Cook time: 6 hours | Serves 8

2 onions, chopped
6 garlic cloves, minced
4 large tomatoes, seeded and chopped
2 dried red chilies, crushed
1 jalapeño pepper, minced

2 tablespoons chili powder
3 tablespoons cocoa powder
2 tablespoons coconut sugar
½ cup chicken stock
6 (5-ounce / 142-g) boneless, skinless chicken breasts

1. In a 6-quart crock pot, mix the onions, garlic, tomatoes, chili peppers, and jalapeño peppers. 2. In a medium bowl, mix the chili powder, cocoa powder, coconut sugar, and chicken stock. 3. Cut the chicken breasts into 1-inch strips crosswise and add to the crock pot. Pour the chicken stock mixture over all. 4. Cover and cook on low for 4 to 6 hours, or until the chicken registers 165°F (74°C) on a food thermometer. Serve with toothpicks or little plates and forks.

Spiced Nut Mix

Prep time: 20 minutes | Cook time: 3 hours | Makes
12 cups

3 cups raw cashews
3 cups walnuts
3 cups pecans
3 cups macadamia nuts
¼ cup melted unsalted butter

½ cup coconut sugar
2 tablespoons chili powder
2 teaspoons paprika
¼ teaspoon cayenne pepper

1. In a 6-quart crock pot, mix the cashews, walnuts, pecans, and macadamia nuts. Drizzle with the melted butter and toss. 2. In a small bowl, mix the coconut sugar, chili powder, paprika, and cayenne pepper until well combined. Sprinkle over the nuts and toss. 3. Partially cover the crock pot and cook on low for 2 to 3 hours, stirring twice during cooking time, until the nuts are golden and toasted.

Caramelized Onion Dip

Prep time: 20 minutes | Cook time: 10½ hours |
Serves 12

2 white onions, chopped
3 onions, sliced
2 cups sliced cremini mushrooms
6 garlic cloves, minced
2 tablespoons unsalted butter

1 bay leaf
1 teaspoon dried thyme leaves
2 tablespoons balsamic vinegar
2½ cups grated Gruyère cheese
2 tablespoons cornstarch

1. In a 6-quart crock pot, mix the onions, mushrooms, garlic, butter, bay leaf, thyme, and balsamic vinegar. 2. Cover and cook on low for 8 to 10 hours, or until the onions are deep golden brown and very soft. Remove and discard the bay leaf. 3. Toss the cheese with the cornstarch in a medium bowl and then add to the crock pot. 4. Cover and cook on low for another 20 to 30 minutes, or until the cheese has melted. 5. Serve with crudités and tortilla chips.

Chapter 6 Fish and Seafood

Scallop and Crab Cioppino

Prep time: 15 minutes | Cook time: 6½ hours |
Serves 4

Cooking oil spray
1 medium yellow onion, finely chopped
4 cloves garlic, minced
1 (15-ounce / 425-g) can diced tomatoes, with the juice
1 (10-ounce / 283-g0 can diced tomatoes with green chiles
2 cups seafood stock
1 cup red wine

3 tablespoons chopped fresh basil
2 bay leaves
1 pound (454 g) cooked crabmeat, shredded
1½ pounds (680 g) scallops
Sea salt
Black pepper
¼ cup fresh flat-leaf parsley, for garnish

1. Coat a large sauté pan with cooking oil spray and heat over medium-high heat. Add the onion and sauté for about 5 minutes, until softened. 2. Add the garlic and sauté until golden and fragrant, about 2 minutes. 3. Transfer the onion and garlic to the crock pot, and add the tomatoes, tomatoes with green chiles, stock, wine, basil, and bay leaves. Cover and cook on low for 6 hours. 4. About 30 minutes before the cooking time is completed, add the crabmeat and scallops. Cover and cook on high for 30 minutes. The seafood will turn opaque. Season to taste with salt and pepper. Serve hot, garnished with parsley.

Simple Poached Turbot

Prep time: 10 minutes | Cook time: 50 minutes |
Serves 4

1 cup vegetable or chicken stock
½ cup dry white wine
1 yellow onion, sliced

1 lemon, sliced
4 sprigs fresh dill
½ teaspoon sea salt
4 (6-ounce / 170-g) turbot fillets

1. Combine the stock and wine in the crock pot. Cover and heat on high for 20 to 30 minutes. 2. Add the onion, lemon, dill, salt, and turbot to the crock pot. Cover and cook on high for about 20 minutes, until the turbot is opaque and cooked through according to taste. Serve hot.

Shrimp with Marinara Sauce

Prep time: 15 minutes | Cook time: 6 to 7 hours |
Serves 4

1 (15-ounce / 425-g) can diced tomatoes, with the juice
1 (6-ounce / 170-g) can tomato paste
1 clove garlic, minced
2 tablespoons minced fresh flat-leaf parsley
½ teaspoon dried basil
1 teaspoon dried oregano

1 teaspoon garlic powder
1½ teaspoons sea salt
¼ teaspoon black pepper
1 pound (454 g) cooked shrimp, peeled and deveined
2 cups hot cooked spaghetti or linguine, for serving
½ cup grated parmesan cheese, for serving

1. Combine the tomatoes, tomato paste, and minced garlic in the crock pot. Sprinkle with the parsley, basil, oregano, garlic powder, salt, and pepper. 2. Cover and cook on low for 6 to 7 hours. 3. Turn up the heat to high, stir in the cooked shrimp, and cover and cook on high for about 15 minutes longer. 4. Serve hot over the cooked pasta. Top with Parmesan cheese.

Citrus Swordfish

Prep time: 10 minutes | Cook time: 1½ hours |
Serves 2

Nonstick cooking oil spray
1½ pounds (680 g) swordfish fillets
Sea salt
Black pepper
1 yellow onion, chopped
5 tablespoons chopped fresh

flat-leaf parsley
1 tablespoon olive oil
2 teaspoons lemon zest
2 teaspoons orange zest
Orange and lemon slices, for garnish
Fresh parsley sprigs, for garnish

1. Coat the interior of the crock pot crock with nonstick cooking oil spray. 2. Season the fish fillets with salt and pepper. Place the fish in the crock pot. 3. Distribute the onion, parsley, olive oil, lemon zest, and orange zest over fish. 4. Cover and cook on low for 1½ hours. 5. Serve hot, garnished with orange and lemon slices and sprigs of fresh parsley.

Shrimp and Fish Chowder

Prep time: 20 minutes | Cook time: 4 to 6 hours |
Serves 4

3 cups low-sodium vegetable broth
1 (28-ounce / 794-g) can no-salt-added crushed tomatoes
1 large bell pepper, any color, seeded and diced
1 large onion, diced
2 zucchini, chopped
3 garlic cloves, minced
1 teaspoon dried thyme

1 teaspoon dried basil
½ teaspoon sea salt
¼ teaspoon freshly ground black pepper
¼ teaspoon red pepper flakes
8 ounces (227 g) whole raw medium shrimp, peeled and deveined
8 ounces (227 g) fresh cod fillets, cut into 1-inch pieces

1. In a crock pot, combine the vegetable broth, tomatoes, bell pepper, onion, zucchini, garlic, thyme, basil, salt, black pepper, and red pepper flakes. Stir to mix well. 2. Cover the cooker and cook for 4 to 6 hours on Low heat. 3. Stir in the shrimp and cod. Replace the cover on the cooker and cook for 15 to 30 minutes on Low heat, or until the shrimp have turned pink and the cod is firm and flaky.

Red Snapper with Peppers and Potatoes

Prep time: 15 minutes | Cook time: 4 to 6 hours |
Serves 4

1 pound (454 g) red potatoes, chopped
1 green bell pepper, seeded and sliced
1 red bell pepper, seeded and sliced
½ onion, sliced
1 (15-ounce / 425-g) can no-salt-added diced tomatoes
⅓ cup whole Kalamata olives, pitted

5 garlic cloves, minced
1 teaspoon dried thyme
1 teaspoon dried rosemary
Juice of 1 lemon
Sea salt
Freshly ground black pepper
1½ to 2 pounds (680 to 907 g) fresh red snapper fillets
2 lemons, thinly sliced
¼ cup chopped fresh parsley

1. In a crock pot, combine the potatoes, green and red bell peppers, onion, tomatoes, olives, garlic, thyme, rosemary, and lemon juice. Season with salt and black pepper. Stir to mix well. 2. Nestle the snapper into the vegetable mixture in a single layer, cutting it into pieces to fit if needed. Top it with lemon slices. 3. Cover the cooker and cook for 4 to 6 hours on Low heat, or until the potatoes are tender. 4. Garnish with fresh parsley for serving.

Shrimp Risotto

Prep time: 10 minutes | Cook time: 4 to 6 hours |
Serves 4

1½ cups raw arborio rice
4½ cups low-sodium chicken broth
½ cup diced onion
2 garlic cloves, minced
½ teaspoon sea salt
½ teaspoon dried parsley

¼ teaspoon freshly ground black pepper
1 pound (454 g) whole raw medium shrimp, peeled and deveined
¼ cup grated Parmesan cheese

1. In a crock pot, combine the rice, chicken broth, onion, garlic, salt, parsley, and pepper. Stir to mix well. 2. Cover the cooker and cook for 4 to 6 hours on Low heat. 3. Stir in the shrimp and Parmesan cheese. Replace the cover on the cooker and cook for 15 to 30 minutes on Low heat, or until the shrimp have turned pink and the cheese is melted.

Shrimp Foil Packets

Prep time: 15 minutes | Cook time: 4 to 6 hours |
Serves 4

1½ pounds (680 g) whole raw medium shrimp, peeled, deveined, and divided into 4 (6-ounce / 170-g) portions
Sea salt
Freshly ground black pepper
2 teaspoons extra-virgin olive oil, divided
4 teaspoons balsamic vinegar,

divided
4 garlic cloves, minced
1 red onion, cut into chunks
1 large zucchini, sliced
4 Roma tomatoes, chopped
4 teaspoons dried oregano, divided
Juice of 1 lemon

1. Place a large sheet of aluminum foil on a work surface. Lay one-quarter of the shrimp in the center of the foil and season it with salt and pepper. Drizzle with ½ teaspoon of olive oil and 1 teaspoon of vinegar. 2. Top the shrimp with one-quarter each of the garlic, onion, and zucchini, plus 1 tomato and 1 teaspoon of oregano. Place a second sheet of foil on top of the ingredients. Fold the corners over to seal the packet. 3. Repeat to make 3 more foil packets. Place the packets in a crock pot in a single layer, or stack them if needed. 4. Cover the cooker and cook for 4 to 6 hours on Low heat. 5. Be careful when serving: Very hot steam will release when you open the foil packets. Drizzle each opened packet with lemon juice for serving.

Creole Crayfish

Prep time: 10 minutes | Cook time: 3 to 4 hours | Serves 2

1½ cups diced celery	juice
1 large yellow onion, chopped	1 clove garlic, minced
2 small bell peppers, any colors, chopped	½ teaspoon sea salt
1 (8-ounce / 227-g) can tomato sauce	¼ teaspoon black pepper
1 (28-ounce / 794-g) can whole tomatoes, broken up, with the	6 drops hot pepper sauce (like tabasco)
	1 pound (454 g) precooked crayfish meat

1. Place the celery, onion, and bell peppers in the crock pot. Add the tomato sauce, tomatoes, and garlic. Sprinkle with the salt and pepper and add the hot sauce. 2. Cover and cook on high for 3 to 4 hours or on low for 6 to 8 hours. 3. About 30 minutes before the cooking time is completed, add the crayfish. 4. Serve hot.

Spicy Tomato Basil Mussels

Prep time: 20 minutes | Cook time: 5½ hours | Serves 4

3 tablespoons olive oil	¾ cup white wine
4 cloves garlic, minced	2 tablespoons dried oregano
3 shallot cloves, minced	½ tablespoon dried basil
8 ounces (227 g) mushrooms, diced	½ teaspoon black pepper
	1 teaspoon paprika
1 (28-ounce / 794-g) can diced tomatoes, with the juice	¼ teaspoon red pepper flakes
	3 pounds (1.4 kg) mussels

1. In a large sauté pan, heat the olive oil over medium-high heat. Cook the garlic, shallots, and mushrooms for 2 to 3 minutes, until the garlic is just a bit brown and fragrant. Scrape the entire contents of the pan into the crock pot. 2. Add the tomatoes and white wine to the crock pot. Sprinkle with the oregano, basil, black pepper, paprika, and red pepper flakes. 3. Cover and cook on low for 4 to 5 hours, or on high for 2 to 3 hours. The mixture is done cooking when mushrooms are fork tender. 4. Clean and debeard the mussels. Discard any open mussels. 5. Increase the heat on the crock pot to high once the mushroom mixture is done. Add the cleaned mussels to the crock pot and secure the lid tightly. Cook for 30 more minutes. 6. To serve, ladle the mussels into bowls with plenty of broth. Discard any mussels that didn't open up during cooking. Serve hot, with crusty bread for sopping up the sauce.

Low Country Seafood Boil

Prep time: 15 minutes | Cook time: 6 hours | Serves 8

8 medium red potatoes	10 cups water
2 large, sweet onions, such as Vidalia, quartered	4 ears of corn, halved
2 pounds (907 g) smoked sausage, cut into 3-inch pieces	2 pounds (907 g) medium raw shrimp, shelled and deveined
1 (3-ounce / 85-g) package seafood boil seasoning	Cocktail sauce, for serving
	Hot sauce, for serving
1 (12-ounce / 340-g) bottle pale ale beer	½ cup melted butter, for serving
	1 large lemon, cut into wedges, for garnish

1. In the crock pot, put the potatoes, onions, smoked sausage, seafood boil seasoning, beer, and water. Stir to combine. Cover and cook for 6 hours, or until the potatoes are tender when pierced with a fork. 2. About 45 minutes before serving, add the corn. Cover and continue cooking for 25 minutes. Add the shrimp, cover, and continue cooking until the shrimp are pink and no longer translucent. 3. Drain the crock pot, discard the cooking liquid, and serve the seafood with cocktail sauce, hot sauce, melted butter, and lemon wedges.

Moroccan Fish

Prep time: 10 minutes | Cook time: 2 to 4 hours | Serves 4

Ras Al-Hanout:	⅛ teaspoon ground cloves
¼ teaspoon ground cumin	⅛ teaspoon sea salt
¼ teaspoon ground ginger	⅛ teaspoon freshly ground
¼ teaspoon ground turmeric	black pepper
¼ teaspoon paprika	Fish:
¼ teaspoon garlic powder	Nonstick cooking spray
¼ teaspoon red pepper flakes	2 pounds (907 g) fresh white-fleshed fish fillets of your
⅛ teaspoon ground cinnamon	choice
⅛ teaspoon ground coriander	2 garlic cloves, minced
⅛ teaspoon ground nutmeg	

Make the Ras Al-Hanout: In a small bowl, stir together the cumin, ginger, turmeric, paprika, garlic powder, red pepper flakes, cinnamon, coriander, nutmeg, cloves, salt, and pepper. Make the Fish: 1. Coat a slow-cooker insert with cooking spray, or line the bottom and sides with parchment paper or aluminum foil. 2. Season the fish all over with the ras al-hanout and garlic. Place the fish in the prepared crock pot in a single layer, cutting it into pieces to fit if needed. 3. Cover the cooker and cook for 2 to 4 hours on Low heat.

Honeyed Salmon

Prep time: 10 minutes | Cook time: 1 hour | Serves 6

6 (6-ounce / 170-g) salmon fillets
½ cup honey
2 tablespoons lime juice
3 tablespoons worcestershire
sauce
1 tablespoon water
2 cloves garlic, minced
1 teaspoon ground ginger
½ teaspoon black pepper

1. Place the salmon fillets in the crock pot. 2. In medium bowl, whisk the honey, lime juice, Worcestershire sauce, water, garlic, ginger, and pepper. Pour sauce over salmon. 3. Cover and cook on high for 1 hour.

Tomato-Basil Salmon

Prep time: 10 minutes | Cook time: 4 to 6 hours | Serves 4

1 (15-ounce / 425-g) can no-salt-added crushed tomatoes
½ cup chopped onion
4 teaspoons dried basil
3 garlic cloves, minced
2 pounds (907 g) fresh salmon
fillets, skin on or off as preferred
1 teaspoon sea salt
¼ teaspoon freshly ground black pepper
¼ cup chopped fresh basil

1. In a crock pot, combine the tomatoes, onion, basil, and garlic. Stir to mix well. 2. Season the salmon all over with salt and pepper. Add the salmon to the crock pot, cutting it into pieces to fit if needed, and spoon some of the tomato mixture on top. 3. Cover the cooker and cook for 4 to 6 hours on Low heat. 4. Garnish with fresh basil for serving.

Fish Chili

Prep time: 10 minutes | Cook time: 5 to 7 hours | Serves 6

1 (28-ounce / 794-g) can no-salt-added diced tomatoes
1 (15-ounce / 425-g) can reduced sodium white beans, drained and rinsed
1 (10-ounce / 283-g) can no-salt-added diced tomatoes with green chiles
1 (8-ounce / 227-g) can no-salt-
added tomato sauce
3 garlic cloves, minced
1 small onion, diced
1 bell pepper, any color, seeded and diced
2 tablespoons chili powder
2 teaspoons ground cumin
1½ teaspoons paprika
1 teaspoon sea salt

1 teaspoon dried oregano
2 pounds (907 g) fresh or frozen
fish fillets of your choice, cut into 2-inch pieces

1. In a crock pot, combine the tomatoes, beans, tomatoes with green chiles, tomato sauce, garlic, onion, bell pepper, chili powder, cumin, paprika, salt, and oregano. Stir to mix well. 2. Cover the cooker and cook for 5 to 7 hours on Low heat. 3. Stir in the fish, replace the cover on the cooker, and cook for 30 minutes on Low heat.

Sesame-Ginger Cod

Prep time: 10 minutes | Cook time: 4 to 6 hours | Serves 4

¼ cup low-sodium soy sauce
2 tablespoons balsamic vinegar
1 tablespoon freshly squeezed lemon juice
2 teaspoons extra-virgin olive oil
1 tablespoon ground ginger
½ teaspoon sea salt
¼ teaspoon freshly ground black pepper
Nonstick cooking spray
2 pounds (907 g) fresh cod fillets
½ teaspoon sesame seeds
4 scallions, green parts only, cut into 3-inch lengths

1. In a small bowl, whisk together the soy sauce, vinegar, lemon juice, olive oil, ginger, salt, and pepper until combined. Set aside. 2. Coat a slow-cooker insert with cooking spray and place the cod in the prepared crock pot. Pour the soy sauce mixture over the cod. 3. Cover the cooker and cook for 4 to 6 hours on Low heat. 4. Garnish with sesame seeds and scallions for serving.

Herbed Tuna Steaks

Prep time: 10 minutes | Cook time: 4 to 6 hours | Serves 4

Nonstick cooking spray
4 (1-inch-thick) fresh tuna steaks (about 2 pounds / 907 g total)
1 teaspoon sea salt
¼ teaspoon freshly ground
black pepper
2 teaspoons extra-virgin olive oil
2 teaspoons dried thyme
2 teaspoons dried rosemary

1. Coat a slow-cooker insert with cooking spray, or line the bottom and sides with parchment paper or aluminum foil. 2. Season the tuna steaks all over with salt and pepper and place them in the prepared crock pot in a single layer. Drizzle with the olive oil and sprinkle with the thyme and rosemary. 3. Cover the cooker and cook for 4 to 6 hours on Low heat.

Seasoned Sole

Prep time: 5 minutes | Cook time: 2 to 4 hours | Serves 4

Nonstick cooking spray

2 pounds (907 g) fresh sole fillets

3 tablespoons freshly squeezed lime juice

2 tablespoons extra-virgin olive oil

2 garlic cloves, minced

1 tablespoon ground cumin

1½ teaspoons paprika

1 teaspoon sea salt

¼ cup fresh cilantro

1. Coat a slow-cooker insert with cooking spray, or line the bottom and sides with parchment paper or aluminum foil. 2. Place the sole in the prepared crock pot in a single layer, cutting it into pieces to fit if needed. 3. In a small bowl, whisk together the lime juice, olive oil, garlic, cumin, paprika, and salt until blended. Pour the sauce over the fish. 4. Cover the cooker and cook for 2 to 4 hours on Low heat. 5. Garnish with fresh cilantro for serving.

Italian Baccalà

Prep time: 2 to 3 hours | Cook time: 4 to 6 hours | Serves 4

1½ pounds (680 g) salt cod

1 (15-ounce / 425-g) can no-salt-added diced tomatoes

½ onion, chopped

2 garlic cloves, minced

½ teaspoon red pepper flakes

¼ cup chopped fresh parsley, plus more for garnish

Juice of ½ lemon

1. Wash the salt cod to remove any visible salt. Completely submerge the cod in a large bowl of water and let it soak for at least 2 to 3 hours. If you are soaking it for longer than 24 hours, change the water after 12 hours. 2. In a crock pot, combine the tomatoes, onion, garlic, red pepper flakes, parsley, and lemon juice. Stir to mix well. Drain the cod and add it to the crock pot, breaking it apart as necessary to make it fit. 3. Cover the cooker and cook for 4 to 6 hours on Low heat. 4. Garnish with the remaining fresh parsley for serving.

Smoked Salmon and Potato Casserole

Prep time: 10 minutes | Cook time: 8 hours | Serves 2

1 teaspoon butter, at room temperature, or extra-virgin olive oil

2 eggs

1 cup 2% milk

1 teaspoon dried dill

⅛ teaspoon sea salt

Freshly ground black pepper

2 medium russet potatoes, peeled and sliced thin

4 ounces (113 g) smoked salmon

1. Grease the inside of the crock pot with the butter. 2. In a small bowl, whisk together the eggs, milk, dill, salt, and a few grinds of the black pepper. 3. Spread one-third of the potatoes in a single layer on the bottom of the crock pot and top them with one-third of the salmon. Pour one-third of the egg mixture over the salmon. Repeat this layering with the remaining potatoes, salmon, and egg mixture. 4. Cover and cook on low for 8 hours or overnight.

Chapter 7 Vegetables and Sides

Creole Green Beans

Prep time: 10 minutes | Cook time: 3 to 4 hours | Serves 4 to 6

2 small onions, chopped
Half a stick butter
4 cups green beans, fresh or frozen

½ cup salsa
2 to 3 tablespoons brown sugar
½ teaspoon garlic salt (optional)

1. Sauté onions in butter in a saucepan. 2. Combine with remaining ingredients in crock pot. 3. Cover and cook on low 3 to 4 hours, or longer, depending upon how soft or crunchy you like your beans.

Golden Carrots

Prep time: 5 minutes | Cook time: 3 to 4 hours | Serves 6

1 (2-pound / 907-g) package baby carrots
½ cup golden raisins
1 stick butter, melted or softened

⅓ cup honey
2 tablespoons lemon juice
½ teaspoon ground ginger (optional)

1. Combine all ingredients in crock pot. 2. Cover and cook on low 3 to 4 hours, or until carrots are tender-crisp.

Cheese Potatoes and Croutons

Prep time: 15 minutes | Cook time: 8¼ hours | Serves 10

6 potatoes, peeled and cut into ¼-inch strips
2 cups sharp Cheddar cheese, shredded
1 (10¾-ounce / 305-g) can cream of chicken soup
1 small onion, chopped

7 tablespoons butter, melted, divided
1 teaspoon salt
1 teaspoon pepper
1 cup sour cream
2 cups seasoned stuffing cubes

1. Toss together potatoes and cheese. Place in crock pot. 2. Combine soup, onion, 4 tablespoons butter, salt, and pepper. Pour over potatoes. 3. Cover. Cook on low 8 hours. 4. Stir in sour cream. Cover and heat for 10 more minutes. 5. Meanwhile, toss together stuffing cubes and 3 tablespoons butter. Sprinkle over potatoes just before serving.

Glazed Root Vegetable Medley

Prep time: 20 minutes | Cook time: 3 hours | Serves 6

2 medium parsnips
4 medium carrots
1 turnip, about 4½ inches around
½ cup water

1 teaspoon salt
½ cup sugar
3 tablespoons butter
½ teaspoon salt

1. Clean and peel vegetables. Cut in 1-inch pieces. 2. Dissolve salt in water in saucepan. Add vegetables and boil for 10 minutes. Drain, reserving ½ cup liquid. 3. Place vegetables in crock pot. Add liquid. 4. Stir in sugar, butter, and salt. 5. Cover. Cook on low 3 hours.

Creamy Mashed Potatoes

Prep time: 15 minutes | Cook time: 3 to 5 hours | Serves 10 to 12

2 teaspoons salt
6 tablespoons (¾ stick) butter, melted
2¼ cups milk
6⅞ cups potato flakes

6 cups water
1 cup sour cream
4 to 5 ounces (113 to 142 g) cream cheese, softened

1. Combine first five ingredients as directed on potato box. 2. Whip cream cheese with electric mixer until creamy. Blend in sour cream. 3. Fold potatoes into cheese and sour cream. Beat well. Place in crock pot. 4. Cover. Cook on low 3 to 5 hours.

Squash and Apples

Prep time: 25 minutes | Cook time: 6 to 8 hours |
Serves 6

1 large butternut squash, peeled, seeded, and cut into ¼-inch slices	3 tablespoons raisins (optional)
	3 tablespoons reduced-calorie pancake syrup
2 medium cooking apples, cored and cut into ¼-inch slices	¼ cup apple cider or apple juice

1. Layer half of the following ingredients in crock pot: squash, apples, and raisins. 2. Drizzle with half the syrup. 3. Repeat layers. 4. Pour cider over the top. 5. Cook on low 6 to 8 hours, or until squash is tender.

Squash Casserole

Prep time: 15 minutes | Cook time: 7 to 9 hours |
Serves 4 to 6

2 pounds (907 g) yellow summer squash or zucchini thinly sliced (about 6 cups)	soup
	1 cup sour cream
	¼ cup flour
Half a medium onion, chopped	1 (8-ounce / 227-g) package seasoned stuffing crumbs
1 cup peeled, shredded carrot	½ cup butter, melted
1 (10¾-ounce / 305-g) can condensed cream of chicken	

1. Combine squash, onion, carrots, and soup. 2. Mix together sour cream and flour. Stir into vegetables. 3. Toss stuffing crumbs with butter. Spread half in bottom of crock pot. Add vegetable mixture. Top with remaining crumbs. 4. Cover. Cook on low 7 to 9 hours.

Purely Artichokes

Prep time: 15 minutes | Cook time: 6 to 8 hours |
Serves 4 to 6

4 to 6 artichokes	2 cups hot water
1 to 1½ teaspoons salt	1 stick (½ cup) butter, melted
1 cup lemon juice, divided	

1. Wash and trim artichokes. Cut off about 1 inch from top. If you wish, trim tips of leaves. Stand chokes upright in crock pot. 2. Sprinkle each choke with ¼ teaspoon salt and 2 tablespoons lemon juice. 3. Pour 2 cups hot water around the base of the artichokes. 4. Cover and cook on low 6 to 8 hours. 5. Serve with melted butter and lemon juice for dipping.

Sweet Potato Stuffing

Prep time: 15 minutes | Cook time: 4 hours | Serves 8

½ cup chopped celery	½ cup chicken broth
½ cup chopped onions	¼ cup chopped pecans
¼ cup butter	½ teaspoon poultry seasoning
6 cups dry bread cubes	½ teaspoon rubbed sage
1 large sweet potato, cooked, peeled, and cubed	½ teaspoon salt
	¼ teaspoon pepper

1. Sauté celery and onion in skillet in butter until tender. Pour into greased crock pot. 2. Add remaining ingredients. Toss gently. 3. Cover. Cook on low 4 hours.

Broccoli Casserole

Prep time: 10 minutes | Cook time: 3 to 5 hours |
Serves 6

1 (10-ounce / 283-g) package frozen chopped broccoli	6 tablespoons flour
	8 ounces (227 g) fat-free mild cheese of your choice, diced
6 eggs, beaten	
(24-ounce / 680-g) carton fat-free small-curd cottage cheese	2 green onions, chopped
	½ teaspoon salt

1. Place frozen broccoli in colander. Run cold water over it until it thaws. Separate into pieces. Drain well. 2. Combine remaining ingredients in large bowl and mix until well blended. Stir in broccoli. Pour into crock pot sprayed with fat-free cooking spray. 3. Cover. Cook on high 1 hour. Stir well, then resume cooking on low 2 to 4 hours.

Zucchini Casserole

Prep time: 20 minutes | Cook time: 4 to 6 hours |
Serves 6

2 to 3 cups thinly sliced zucchini	fat free cream of celery soup
	1 (10¾-ounce / 305-g) can condensed cream of chicken soup
1 medium onion, diced	
2 large carrots, shredded (enough to make 1 cup)	
	¼ teaspoon salt
1 (10¾-ounce / 305-g) can 98%	Fat-free cooking spray

1. Spray crock pot with fat-free cooking spray. Mix vegetables, soups, and salt together gently in crock pot. Cover. 2. Cook on high 4 to 6 hours, or until vegetables are as crunchy or as soft as you like.

Easy Flavor-Filled Green Beans

Prep time: 10 minutes | Cook time: 3 to 4 hours | Serves 10

2 quarts green beans, drained
⅓ cup chopped onions
1 (4-ounce / 113-g) can mushrooms, drained

2 tablespoons brown sugar
3 tablespoons butter
Pepper to taste

1. Combine beans, onions, and mushrooms in crock pot. 2. Sprinkle with brown sugar. 3. Dot with butter. 4. Sprinkle with pepper. 5. Cover. Cook on high 3 to 4 hours. Stir just before serving.

Do-Ahead Mashed Potatoes

Prep time: 45 minutes | Cook time: 3 to 4 hours | Serves 8

12 medium potatoes, washed, peeled, and quartered
1 small or medium onion, chopped
4 ounces (113 g) fat-free cream

cheese
1 teaspoon salt
¼ teaspoon black pepper
1 cup skim milk

1. In a saucepan, cover potatoes and onion with water. Bring to a boil, and then simmer over medium-low heat for 30 minutes or so, until fully softened. Drain. 2. Mash potatoes and onion with a potato masher to remove chunks. 3. In a large mixing bowl, combine partially mashed potatoes, cream cheese, salt, pepper, and milk. Whip together on high for 3 minutes. 4. Transfer potatoes into crock pot. 5. Cook on low 3 to 4 hours.

Cheesy Hominy from Scratch

Prep time: 10 minutes | Cook time: 4 to 9 hours | Serves 12 to 14

2 cups cracked hominy
6 cups water
2 tablespoons flour
1½ cups milk
4 cups shredded sharp Cheddar

cheese
1 to 2 teaspoons salt
¼ teaspoon pepper
4 tablespoons butter

1. Combine hominy and water in 5 to 6 quart crock pot. 2. Cover. Cook on high 3 to 4 hours, or on low 6 to 8 hours. 3. Stir in remaining ingredients. 4. Cover. Cook 30 to 60 minutes.

Stewed Tomatoes

Prep time: 10 minutes | Cook time: 3 to 4 hours | Serves 12

2 quarts low-sodium canned tomatoes
¼ cup sugar
1 teaspoon salt

Dash of black pepper
2 tablespoons butter
2 cups bread cubes

1. Place tomatoes in crock pot. 2. Sprinkle with sugar, salt, and pepper. 3. Lightly toast bread cubes in melted butter in skillet on top of stove. Spread over tomatoes. 4. Cover. Cook on high 3 to 4 hours

Apricot-Glazed Carrots

Prep time: 5 minutes | Cook time: 9¼ hours | Serves 8

2 pounds (907 g) baby carrots
1 onion, chopped
½ cup water
⅓ cup honey

⅓ cup apricot preserves
2 tablespoons chopped fresh parsley

1. Place carrots and onions in crock pot. Add water. 2. Cover and cook on low 9 hours. 3. Drain liquid from crock pot. 4. In a small bowl, mix honey and preserves together. Pour over carrots. 5. Cover and cook on high 10 to 15 minutes. 6. Sprinkle with parsley before serving.

Wild Mushrooms Italian

Prep time: 20 minutes | Cook time: 6 to 8 hours | Serves 5 to 7

2 large onions, chopped
3 large red bell peppers, chopped
3 large green bell peppers, chopped
2 tablespoons oil
1 (12-ounce / 340-g) package oyster mushrooms, cleaned and chopped

4 garlic cloves, minced
3 fresh bay leaves
10 fresh basil leaves, chopped
1½ teaspoons salt
1½ teaspoons black pepper
1 (28-ounce / 794-g) can low-sodium Italian plum tomatoes, crushed or chopped

1. Sauté onions and peppers in oil in skillet until soft. Stir in mushrooms and garlic. Sauté just until mushrooms begin to turn brown. Pour into crock pot. 2. Add remaining ingredients. Stir well. 3. Cover. Cook on low 6 to 8 hours.

Stuffed Peppers with Beans

Prep time: 15 minutes | Cook time: 6 hours | Serves 4

4 medium green, yellow, or red sweet peppers, or a mixture of colors
1 cup rice, cooked
1 (15-ounce / 425-g) can chili

beans with chili gravy
1 cup shredded cheese, divided
1 (14½-ounce / 411-g) can petite diced tomatoes, with onion, celery, and green pepper

1. Wash and dry sweet peppers. Remove tops, membranes, and seeds, but keep the peppers whole. 2. In a bowl, mix together rice, beans, and half the cheese. Spoon mixture into peppers. 3. Pour tomatoes into crock pot. Place filled peppers on top, keeping them upright. Do not stack the peppers. 4. Cover and cook on high 3 hours. 5. Carefully lift peppers out of cooker and place on a serving platter. Spoon hot tomatoes over top. Sprinkle remaining cheese over peppers.

Vegetables with Pasta

Prep time: 20 minutes | Cook time: 6 hours | Serves 6

2 cups chopped zucchini
½ cup cherry tomatoes, cut in half
Half green or red bell pepper, sliced
Half medium onion, sliced

½ cup sliced fresh mushrooms
4 cloves garlic, minced
1 tablespoon olive oil
1 tablespoon Italian seasoning
1 (8-ounce / 227-g) can tomato sauce

1. Combine all ingredients in crock pot. 2. Cook on low 6 hours, or until vegetables are tender.

Creamy Hash Browns

Prep time: 10 minutes | Cook time: 4 to 5 hours | Serves 14

1 (30-ounce / 850-g) package frozen, diced hash browns
2 cups cubed or shredded cheese of your choice
2 cups sour cream

2 (10¾-ounce / 305-g) cans cream of chicken soup
Half a stick (¼ cup) butter, melted

1. Place hash browns in an ungreased crock pot. 2. Combine remaining ingredients and pour over the potatoes. Mix well. 3. Cover and cook on low 4 to 5 hours, or until potatoes are tender and heated through.

Sweet Potatoes and Apples

Prep time: 15 minutes | Cook time: 6 to 8 hours | Serves 8 to 10

3 large sweet potatoes, peeled and cubed
3 large tart and firm apples, peeled and sliced
½ to ¾ teaspoon salt
⅛ to ¼ teaspoon pepper
1 teaspoon sage

1 teaspoon ground cinnamon
4 tablespoons (½ stick) butter, melted
¼ cup maple syrup
Toasted sliced almonds or chopped pecans (optional)

1. Place half the sweet potatoes in crock pot. Layer in half the apple slices. 2. Mix together seasonings. Sprinkle half over apples. 3. Mix together butter and maple syrup. Spoon half over seasonings. 4. Repeat layers. 5. Cover. Cook on low 6 to 8 hours or until potatoes are soft, stirring occasionally. 6. To add a bit of crunch, sprinkle with toasted almonds or pecans when serving. 7. Serve.

Garlicky Potatoes

Prep time: 10 minutes | Cook time: 5 to 6 hours | Serves 6

6 potatoes, peeled and cubed
6 garlic cloves, minced
¼ cup dried onion, or 1 medium

onion, chopped
2 tablespoons olive oil

1. Combine all ingredients in crock pot. 2. Cook on low 5 to 6 hours, or until potatoes are soft but not turning brown.

Potatoes Perfect

Prep time: 15 minutes | Cook time: 3 to 10 hours | Serves 4 to 6

¼ pound (113 g) bacon, diced and browned until crisp
2 medium onions, thinly sliced
6 to 8 medium potatoes, thinly sliced

½ pound (227 g) Cheddar cheese, thinly sliced
Salt to taste
Pepper to taste
2 to 4 tablespoons butter

1. Layer half of bacon, onions, potatoes, and cheese in greased crock pot. Season with salt and pepper to taste. 2. Dot with butter. Repeat layers. 3. Cover. Cook on low 8 to 10 hours, or on high 3 to 4 hours, or until potatoes are soft.

Eggplant Italian

Prep time: 20 minutes | Cook time: 4 hours | Serves 6 to 8

2 eggplants
¼ cup eggbeaters
24 ounces (680 g) fat-free cottage cheese
¼ teaspoon salt
Black pepper to taste

1 (14-ounce / 397-g) tomato sauce
2 to 4 tablespoons Italian seasoning, according to your taste preference

1. Peel eggplants and cut in ½-inch-thick slices. Soak in salt-water for about 5 minutes to remove bitterness. Drain well. 2. Spray crock pot with fat-free cooking spray. 3. Mix eggbeaters, cottage cheese, salt, and pepper together in bowl. 4. Mix tomato sauce and Italian seasoning together in another bowl. 5. Spoon a thin layer of tomato sauce into bottom of crock pot. Top with about one-third of the eggplant slices, and then one-third of the egg-cheese mixture, and finally one-third of the remaining tomato sauce mixture. 6. Repeat those layers twice, ending with seasoned tomato sauce. 7. Cover. Cook on high 4 hours. Allow to rest 15 minutes before serving.

Corn on the Cob

Prep time: 10 minutes | Cook time: 2 to 3 hours | Serves 3 to 4

6 to 8 ears of corn (in husk)   ½ cup water

1. Remove silk from corn, as much as possible, but leave husks on. 2. Cut off ends of corn so ears can stand in the cooker. 3. Add water. 4. Cover. Cook on low 2 to 3 hours.

Lemon Red Potatoes

Prep time: 10 minutes | Cook time: 2½ to 3 hours | Serves 6

1½ pounds (680 g) medium red potatoes
¼ cup water
2 tablespoons butter, melted
1 tablespoon lemon juice

3 tablespoons fresh chives, snipped
Chopped fresh parsley
1 teaspoon salt
½ teaspoon black pepper

1. Cut a strip of peel from around the middle of each potato. Place potatoes and water in crock pot. 2. Cover. Cook on high 2½ to 3 hours. 3. Drain. 4. Combine butter, lemon juice, chives, and parsley. Pour over potatoes. Toss to coat. 5. Season with salt and pepper.

Creamy Scalloped Potatoes

Prep time: 15 minutes | Cook time: 3 to 9 hours | Serves 6

6 large potatoes, peeled and thinly sliced
1 small onion, thinly sliced
¼ cup flour
1 teaspoon salt
¼ teaspoon pepper

2 tablespoons butter, melted
¼ cup milk
1 (10¾-ounce / 305-g) can cream of mushroom soup
4 slices American cheese, or 1 cup shredded Cheddar cheese

1. Place half of potatoes in crock pot. Top with half of onion, flour, salt, and pepper. Repeat layers. 2. Mix together butter, milk, and soup. Pour over potato layers. 3. Cover. Cook on low 6 to 9 hours, or on high 3 to 4 hours, or until potatoes are soft. 4. Add cheese 30 minutes before serving.

Mushrooms in Red Wine

Prep time: 5 minutes | Cook time: 6 hours | Serves 4

1 pound (454 g) fresh mushrooms, stemmed, trimmed, and cleaned
4 cloves garlic, minced

¼ cup onion
1 tablespoon olive oil
1 cup red wine

1. Combine all ingredients in crock pot. 2. Cook on low 6 hours.

Fresh Herb Stuffing

Prep time: 25 minutes | Cook time: 4 to 5 hours | Serves 8

3 tablespoons butter
3 onions, chopped
4 celery ribs, chopped
½ cup chopped fresh parsley
1 tablespoon chopped fresh rosemary
1 tablespoon chopped fresh thyme
1 tablespoon chopped fresh

marjoram
1 tablespoon chopped fresh sage
1 teaspoon salt
½ teaspoon freshly-ground black pepper
1 loaf stale low-fat sourdough bread, cut in 1-inch cubes
2 cups fat-free chicken broth

1. Sauté onions and celery in butter in skillet until transparent. Remove from heat and stir in fresh herbs and seasonings. 2. Place bread cubes in large bowl. Add onion/herb mixture. Add enough broth to moisten. Mix well but gently. Turn into greased crock pot. 3. Cover. Cook on high 1 hour. Reduce heat to low and continue cooking 3 to 4 hours.

Tzimmes

Prep time: 30 minutes | Cook time: 10 hours |
Serves 6 to 8

1 to 2 sweet potatoes	juice
6 carrots, sliced	½ pound (227 g) dried apricots
1 potato, peeled and diced	1 tablespoon ground cinnamon
1 onion, chopped	1 tablespoon apple pie spice
2 apples, peeled and sliced	1 tablespoon maple syrup or
1 butternut squash, peeled and	honey
sliced	1 teaspoon salt
¼ cup dry white wine or apple	1 teaspoon ground ginger

1. Combine all ingredients in large crock pot, or mix all ingredients in large bowl and then divide between 2 (4- to 5-quart) cookers. 2. Cover. Cook on low 10 hours.

Rosy Sweet Potatoes

Prep time: 5 minutes | Cook time: 3 to 4 hours |
Serves 8

1 (40-ounce / 1.1-kg) can	⅓ cup brown sugar
unsweetened sweet potato	⅓ cup red hots
chunks, drained	1 teaspoon ground cinnamon
1 (21-ounce / 595-g) can lite	Nonfat cooking spray
apple pie filling	

1. Combine all ingredients in a large bowl. Pour into crock pot sprayed with nonfat cooking spray. 2. Cover. Cook on low 3 to 4 hours.

Vegetable Rice Casserole

Prep time: 10 minutes | Cook time: 3 to 4 hours |
Serves 8

¼ cup rice, uncooked	4 celery ribs with leaves,
1 pound (454 g) zucchini, sliced	chopped
1 pound (454 g) yellow summer	2 large tomatoes, sliced
squash, sliced	¼ cup packed brown sugar
1 large onion, sliced	½ teaspoon salt
1 tablespoon dried basil,	¼ teaspoon black pepper
divided	2 tablespoons olive oil
1 medium green bell pepper,	Fat-free cooking spray
julienned	

1. Spread rice in crock pot that has been coated with fat-free cooking spray. 2. Layer in zucchini, yellow squash, onion, and half the basil. 3. Top with green pepper, celery, and tomatoes. 4. Combine brown sugar, salt, and pepper. Sprinkle over vegetables. Drizzle with oil. 5. Cover. Cook on high 3 to 4 hours, or until the vegetables reach the degree of "doneness" that you prefer. 6. Sprinkle with remaining basil when finished.

Onion Potatoes

Prep time: 20 minutes | Cook time: 5 to 6 hours |
Serves 6

6 medium potatoes, diced	1 envelope dry onion soup mix
⅓ cup olive oil	

1. Combine potatoes and olive oil in plastic bag. Shake well. 2. Add onion soup mix. Shake well. 3. Pour into crock pot. 4. Cover and cook on low 5 to 6 hours.

Cranberry-Orange Beets

Prep time: 15 minutes | Cook time: 3½ to 7½ hours |
Serves 6

2 pounds (907 g) medium beets,	shredded (optional)
peeled and quartered	2 tablespoons butter
½ teaspoon ground nutmeg	2 tablespoons sugar
1 cup cranberry juice	4 teaspoons cornstarch
1 teaspoon orange peel, finely	

1. Place beets in crock pot. Sprinkle with nutmeg. 2. Add cranberry juice and orange peel. Dot with butter. 3. Cover. Cook on low 6 to 7 hours, or on high 3 to 3½ hours. 4. In small bowl, combine sugar and cornstarch. 5. Remove ½ cup of cooking liquid and stir into cornstarch. 6. Stir mixture into crock pot. 7. Cover. Cook on high 15 to 30 minutes.

"Baked" Corn

Prep time: 5 minutes | Cook time: 3 hours | Serves 8

1 quart corn (be sure to thaw	⅛ teaspoon black pepper
and drain if using frozen corn)	2 teaspoons oil
2 eggs, beaten	2 tablespoons sugar
1 teaspoon salt	3 tablespoons flour
1 cup fat-free milk	

1. Combine all ingredients well. Pour into crock pot sprayed with fat-free cooking spray. 2. Cover. Cook on high 3 hours.

Rustic Potatoes au Gratin

Prep time: 10 minutes | Cook time: 6 to 8 hours | Serves 6

½ cup skim milk
1 (10¾-ounce / 305-g) can light condensed Cheddar cheese soup
1 (8-ounce / 227-g) package fat-free cream cheese, softened
1 clove garlic, minced
¼ teaspoon ground nutmeg

¼ teaspoon black pepper
2 pounds (907 g) baking potatoes, cut into ¼-inch-thick slices
1 small onion, thinly sliced
Paprika
Nonfat cooking spray

1. Heat milk in small saucepan over medium heat until small bubbles form around edge of pan. Remove from heat. 2. Add soup, cream cheese, garlic, nutmeg, and pepper to pan. Stir until smooth. 3. Spray inside of crock pot with nonfat cooking spray. Layer one-quarter of potatoes and onions on bottom of crock pot. 4. Top with one-quarter of soup mixture. Repeat layers 3 times. 5. Cover. Cook on low 6 to 8 hours, or until potatoes are tender and most of liquid is absorbed. 6. Sprinkle with paprika before serving.

"Baked" Sweet Potatoes

Prep time: 10 minutes | Cook time: 4 to 8 hours | Serves 6 to 8

6 to 8 medium sweet potatoes
Salt to taste

Butter, for serving

1. Scrub and prick sweet potatoes with fork. Wrap each in tin foil and arrange in crock pot. 2. Cover. Cook on low 6 to 8 hours, or on high 4 to 5 hours, or until each potato is soft. 3. Remove from foil and serve with butter and salt.

"Baked" Tomatoes

Prep time: 5 minutes | Cook time: ¾ to 1 hour | Serves 4

2 tomatoes, each cut in half
½ tablespoon olive oil
½ teaspoon parsley, chopped, or
¼ teaspoon dry parsley flakes

¼ teaspoon dried oregano
¼ teaspoon dried basil
Nonfat cooking spray

1. Place tomato halves in crock pot sprayed with nonfat cooking spray. 2. Drizzle oil over tomatoes. Sprinkle with remaining ingredients. 3. Cover. Cook on high 45 minutes to 1 hour.

Sweet Potato, Fruit Compote

Prep time: 20 minutes | Cook time: 5 to 6 hours | Serves 8

4 cups sweet potatoes, peeled and cubed
3 tart cooking apples, peeled and diced
1 (20-ounce / 567-g)

unsweetened pineapple chunks, undrained
¼ cup brown sugar
1 cup miniature marshmallows, divided

1. Cook sweet potatoes in a small amount of water in a saucepan until almost soft. Drain. 2. Combine sweet potatoes, apples, and pineapples in crock pot. 3. Sprinkle with brown sugar and ⅔ cup marshmallows. 4. Cover. Cook on low 5 to 6 hours. 5. Thirty minutes before serving, top potatoes and fruit with remaining ⅓ cup marshmallows. Cover and continue cooking.

Uptown Scalloped Potatoes

Prep time: 15 minutes | Cook time: 6 to 7 hours | Serves 8 to 10

5 pounds (2.3 kg) red potatoes, peeled and sliced
2 cups water
1 teaspoon cream of tartar
¼ pound (113 g) bacon, cut in

1-inch squares, browned until crisp, and drained
Dash of salt
½ pint whipping cream
1 pint half-and-half

1. Toss potatoes in water and cream of tartar. Drain. 2. Layer potatoes and bacon in large crock pot. Sprinkle with salt. 3. Mix whipping cream and half-and-half. 4. Cover. Cook on low 6 to 7 hours.

Broccoli Delight

Prep time: 15 minutes | Cook time: 2 to 6 hours | Serves 4 to 6

1 to 2 pounds (454 to 907 g) broccoli, chopped
2 cups cauliflower, chopped
1 (10¾-ounce / 305-g) can 98% fat-free cream of celery soup
½ teaspoon salt

¼ teaspoon black pepper
1 medium onion, diced
2 to 4 garlic cloves, crushed, according to your taste preference
½ cup vegetable broth

1. Combine all ingredients in crock pot. 2. Cook on low 4 to 6 hours, or on high 2 to 3 hours.

crock pot Ratatouille

Prep time: 20 minutes | Cook time: 4 to 7 hours |

Serves 6

1 tablespoon olive oil	¼ cup dry red wine or wine
1 large onion, chopped	vinegar
6 large garlic cloves, minced	1 tablespoon lemon juice
1 green bell pepper, cut into	2 teaspoons dried thyme
strips	1 teaspoon dried oregano
1 red bell pepper, cut into strips	1 teaspoon ground cumin
1 medium eggplant, cubed	½ to 1 teaspoon salt
2 cups thickly sliced	¼ to ½ teaspoon black pepper
mushrooms	4 tablespoons minced fresh
4 tomatoes, cubed	basil
1 cup low-sodium tomato purée	¼ cup chopped fresh parsley

1. Turn crock pot on high for 2 minutes. 2. Pour oil into crock pot and add remaining ingredients except parsley and fresh basil. 3. Cover. Cook on high 2 hours, then on low 4 to 5 hours. 4. Stir in fresh basil. Sprinkle with parsley. Serve.

Sweet Potato Casserole

Prep time: 10 minutes | Cook time: 3 to 4 hours |

Serves 8

2 (29-ounce / 822-g) cans sweet	½ cup fat-free milk
potatoes, drained and mashed	⅓ cup chopped pecans
2 tablespoons brown sugar	⅓ cup brown sugar
1 tablespoon orange juice	2 tablespoons flour
2 eggs, beaten	2 teaspoons butter, melted

1. Combine sweet potatoes and 2 tablespoons brown sugar. 2. Stir in orange juice, eggs, and milk. Transfer to greased crock pot. 3. Combine pecans, ⅓ cup brown sugar, flour, and butter. Spread over sweet potatoes. 4. Cover. Cook on high 3 to 4 hours.

Garlic Mashed Potatoes

Prep time: 20 minutes | Cook time: 4 to 7 hours |

Serves 6

2 pounds (907 g) baking	1 teaspoon salt
potatoes, unpeeled and cut into	¾ teaspoon garlic powder
½-inch cubes	¼ teaspoon black pepper
¼ cup water	1 cup milk
3 tablespoons butter, sliced	

1. Combine all ingredients, except milk, in crock pot. Toss to combine. 2. Cover. Cook on low 7 hours, or on high 4 hours. 3. Add milk to potatoes during last 30 minutes of cooking time. 4. Mash potatoes with potato masher or electric mixer until fairly smooth. 5. Serve immediately.

Cheesy Scalloped Potatoes

Prep time: 15 minutes | Cook time: 3 to 4 hours |

Serves 8 to 10

2 tablespoons dried minced	1 (8-ounce / 227-g) package
onion	cream cheese, cubed, divided
1 medium clove garlic, minced	½ cup shredded Cheddar cheese
1 teaspoon salt	(optional)
8 to 10 medium fresh potatoes,	Nonstick cooking spray
sliced, divided	

1. Spray interior of crock pot with nonstick cooking spray. 2. In a small bowl, combine onion, garlic, and salt. 3. Layer about one-fourth of the potatoes into the crock pot. 4. Sprinkle one-fourth of onion-garlic mixture over potatoes. 5. Spoon about one-third of cream cheese cubes over top. 6. Repeat layers, ending with the seasoning. 7. Cook on high 3 to 4 hours, or until potatoes are tender. 8. Stir potatoes to spread out the cream cheese. If you wish, you can mash the potatoes at this point. 9. If you like, sprinkle shredded cheese over top of the sliced or mashed potatoes. 10. Cover and cook an additional 10 minutes, or until the cheese is melted.

Apple Stuffing

Prep time: 20 minutes | Cook time: 4 to 5 hours |

Serves 4 to 5

1 stick (½ cup) butter, divided	dry herb-seasoned stuffing mix
1 cup chopped walnuts	1½ cups applesauce
2 onions, chopped	Water (optional)
1 (14-ounce / 397-g) package	Nonstick cooking spray

1. In nonstick skillet, melt 2 tablespoons of butter. Sauté walnuts over medium heat until toasted, about 5 minutes, stirring frequently. Remove from skillet and set aside. 2. Melt remaining butter in skillet. Add onions and cook 3 to 4 minutes, or until almost tender. Set aside. 3. Spray crock pot with nonstick cooking spray. Place dry stuffing mix in crock pot. 4. Add onion-butter mixture and stir. Add applesauce and stir. 5. Cover and cook on low 4 to 5 hours, or until heated through. Check after Stuffing has cooked for 3½ hours. If it's sticking to the cooker, drying out, or becoming too brown on the edges, stir in ½ to 1 cup water. Continue cooking. 6. Sprinkle with walnuts before serving.

Refrigerator Mashed Potatoes

Prep time: 30 minutes | Cook time: 2 hours | Serves 8 to 10

5 pounds (2.3 kg) potatoes
1 (8-ounce / 227-g) package cream cheese, softened
1 cup sour cream

1 teaspoon salt
¼ teaspoon pepper
¼ cup crisp bacon, crumbled
2 tablespoons butter

1. Cook and mash potatoes. 2. Add remaining ingredients except butter. Put in crock pot. Dot with butter. 3. Cover. Cook on low 2 hours.

Pizza Potatoes

Prep time: 15 minutes | Cook time: 6 to 10 hours | Serves 4 to 6

6 medium potatoes, sliced
1 large onion, thinly sliced
2 tablespoons olive oil
2 cups shredded Mozzarella cheese

2 ounces (57 g) sliced pepperoni
1 teaspoon salt
1 (8-ounce / 227-g) can pizza sauce

1. Sauté potato and onion slices in oil in skillet until onions appear transparent. Drain well. 2. In crock pot, combine potatoes, onions, cheese, pepperoni, and salt. 3. Pour pizza sauce over top. 4. Cover. Cook on low 6 to 10 hours, or until potatoes are soft.

Fruity Sweet Potatoes

Prep time: 15 minutes | Cook time: 6 to 8 hours | Serves 6

2 pounds (907 g) sweet potatoes or yams
1½ cups applesauce
⅔ cup brown sugar

3 tablespoons butter, melted
1 teaspoon cinnamon
Chopped nuts (optional)

1. Peel sweet potatoes if you wish. Cut into cubes or slices. Place in crock pot. 2. In a bowl, mix together applesauce, brown sugar, butter, and cinnamon. Spoon over potatoes. 3. Cover and cook on low 6 to 8 hours, or until potatoes are tender. 4. Mash potatoes and sauce together if you wish with a large spoon—or spoon potatoes into serving dish and top with the sauce. 5. Sprinkle with nuts, if you want.

Simply Scalloped Potatoes

Prep time: 10 minutes | Cook time: 2 hours | Serves 3 to 4

2 cups thinly sliced raw potatoes, divided
1 tablespoon flour
1 teaspoon salt

Pepper
1 cup milk
1 tablespoon butter
Nonstick cooking spray

1. Spray crock pot with nonstick cooking spray. 2. Put half of thinly sliced potatoes in bottom of crock pot. 3. In a small bowl, mix together flour, salt, and pepper. Sprinkle half over top of potatoes. 4. Repeat layering. 5. Pour milk over all. Dot with butter. 6. Cover and cook on high 2 hours.

Swiss-Irish Hot Sauce

Prep time: 15 minutes | Cook time: 4 hours | Serves 6 to 8

2 medium onions, diced
5 garlic cloves, minced
¼ cup oil
1 (1-pound / 454-g) can tomatoes, puréed
1 (15-ounce / 425-g) can tomato sauce
1 (12-ounce / 340-g) can tomato paste
2 tablespoons parsley, fresh or

dried
½ teaspoon red pepper
½ teaspoon black pepper
1 teaspoon chili powder
1 teaspoon dried basil
2 teaspoons Worcestershire sauce
2 teaspoons Tabasco sauce
¼ cup red wine

1. Sauté onions and garlic in oil in skillet. 2. Combine all ingredients in crock pot. 3. Cover. Cook on low 4 hours. 4. Serve.

Cheesy Corn

Prep time: 10 minutes | Cook time: 4 hours | Serves 10

3 (16-ounce / 454-g) packages frozen corn
1 (8-ounce / 227-g) package cream cheese, cubed
¼ cup butter, cubed

3 tablespoons water
3 tablespoons milk
2 tablespoons sugar
6 slices American cheese, cut into squares

1. Combine all ingredients in crock pot. Mix well. 2. Cover. Cook on low 4 hours, or until heated through and the cheese is melted.

Stuffed Acorn Squash

Prep time: 15 minutes | Cook time: 2½ hours | Serves 6

3 small carnival or acorn squash	3 tablespoons minced onion
5 tablespoons instant brown rice	Pinch of ground or dried sage
3 tablespoons dried cranberries	1 teaspoon butter, divided
3 tablespoons diced celery	3 tablespoons orange juice
	½ cup water

1. Slice off points on the bottoms of squash so they will stand in crock pot. Slice off tops and discard. Scoop out seeds. Place squash in crock pot. 2. Combine rice, cranberries, celery, onion, and sage. Stuff into squash. 3. Dot with butter. 4. Pour 1 tablespoon orange juice into each squash. 5. Pour water into bottom of crock pot. 6. Cover. Cook on low 2½ hours. 7. Serve.

Easy Olive Bake

Prep time: 15 minutes | Cook time: 3 hours | Serves 8

1 cup rice, uncooked	½ teaspoon chili powder
2 medium onions, chopped	1 tablespoon Worcestershire
½ cup butter, melted	sauce
2 cups stewed tomatoes	1 (4-ounce / 113-g) can
2 cups water	mushrooms with juice
1 cup black olives, quartered	½ cup shredded cheese
½ to ¾ teaspoon salt	

1. Wash and drain rice. Place in crock pot. 2. Add remaining ingredients except cheese. Mix well. 3. Cook on high 1 hour, then on low 2 hours, or until rice is tender but not mushy. 4. Add cheese before serving.

Very Special Spinach

Prep time: 10 minutes | Cook time: 5 hours | Serves 8

3 (10-ounce / 283-g) boxes frozen spinach, thawed and drained	3 eggs
	¼ cup flour
2 cups cottage cheese	1 teaspoon salt
1½ cups shredded Cheddar cheese	½ cup butter, or margarine, melted

1. Mix together all ingredients. 2. Pour into crock pot. 3. Cook on high 1 hour. Reduce heat to low and cook 4 more hours.

Parmesan Potato Wedges

Prep time: 15 minutes | Cook time: 4 hours | Serves 6

2 pounds (907 g) red potatoes, cut into ½-inch wedges or strips	pieces
	1½ teaspoons dried oregano
¼ cup chopped onion	¼ cup grated Parmesan cheese
2 tablespoons butter, cut into	

1. Layer potatoes, onion, butter, and oregano in crock pot. 2. Cover and cook on high 4 hours, or until potatoes are tender but not dry or mushy. 3. Spoon into serving dish and sprinkle with cheese.

Mustard Potatoes

Prep time: 5 minutes | Cook time: 2 to 4 hours | Serves 6

½ cup onions, chopped	½ cup fat-free or 2% milk
1 tablespoon butter	¼ pound (113 g) low-fat cheese,
1½ teaspoons prepared mustard	shredded
1 teaspoon salt	6 medium potatoes, cooked and
¼ teaspoon black pepper	grated

1. Sauté onion in butter in skillet. Add mustard, salt, pepper, milk, and cheese. 2. Place potatoes in crock pot. Do not press down. 3. Pour mixture over potatoes. 4. Cover. Cook on low 3 to 4 hours. 5. Toss potatoes with a large spoon when ready to serve.

Cornflake Cooker Potatoes

Prep time: 15 minutes | Cook time: 4 hours | Serves 4 to 6

6 to 8 potatoes, peeled	1 cup cornflakes, slightly crushed
2 teaspoons salt	
2 to 3 tablespoons butter	

1. Place potatoes in crock pot. 2. Fill cooker with hot water. Sprinkle with salt. 3. Cover and cook on high 4 hours, or until potatoes are tender. 4. While potatoes are cooking, melt butter. Continue melting until butter browns, but does not burn. (Watch carefully!) Stir in cornflakes. Set aside. 5. Drain potatoes. Spoon buttered cornflakes over potatoes. or mash potatoes and then top with buttered cornflakes.

Super Green Beans

Prep time: 15 minutes | Cook time: 1 to 2 hours | Serves 5

2 (14½-ounce / 411-g) cans green beans, undrained
1 cup cooked cubed ham

⅓ cup finely chopped onion
1 tablespoon butter, melted, or bacon drippings

1. Place undrained beans in cooker. Add remaining ingredients and mix well. 2. Cook on high 1 to 2 hours, or until steaming hot.

Dried Corn

Prep time: 5 minutes | Cook time: 4 hours | Serves 4

1 (15-ounce / 425-g) can dried corn
2 tablespoons sugar
3 tablespoons butter, softened

1 teaspoon salt
1 cup half-and-half
2 tablespoons water

1.Place all ingredients in crock pot. Mix together well. 2. Cover and cook on low 4 hours. 3. Serve.

Chapter 8 Desserts

Southwest Cranberries

Prep time: 5 minutes | Cook time: 2 to 3 hours | Serves 8

1 (16-ounce / 454-g) can whole berry cranberry sauce
1 (10½-ounce / 298-g) jar

jalapeño jelly
2 tablespoons chopped fresh cilantro

1. Combine ingredients in crock pot. 2. Cover. Cook on low 2 to 3 hours. 3. Cool. Serve at room temperature.

Chunky Cranberry Applesauce

Prep time: 15 minutes | Cook time: 3 to 4 hours | Serves 6

6 baking apple, peeled or unpeeled, cut into 1-inch cubes
½ cup apple juice
½ cup fresh or frozen

cranberries
¼ cup sugar
¼ teaspoon ground cinnamon (optional)

1. Combine all ingredients in crock pot. 2. Cover and cook on low 3 to 4 hours, or until apples are as soft as you like them. 3. Serve warm, or refrigerate and serve chilled.

Scandinavian Fruit Soup

Prep time: 5 minutes | Cook time: 8 hours | Serves 12

1 cup dried apricots
1 cup dried sliced apples
1 cup dried pitted prunes
1 cup canned pitted red cherries
½ cup quick-cooking tapioca
1 cup grape juice or red wine

3 cups water, or more
½ cup orange juice
¼ cup lemon juice
1 tablespoon grated orange peel
½ cup brown sugar

1. Combine apricots, apples, prunes, cherries, tapioca, and grape juice in crock pot. Cover with water. 2. Cook on low for at least 8 hours. 3. Before serving, stir in remaining ingredients. 4. Serve warm or cold.

Bread Pudding

Prep time: 20 minutes | Cook time: 4 to 5 hours | Serves 6

8 slices bread (raisin bread is especially good), cubed
4 eggs
2 cups milk
¼ cup sugar
¼ cup butter, melted
½ cup raisins (use only ¼ cup if using raisin bread)

½ teaspoon cinnamon
Sauce:
2 tablespoons butter
2 tablespoons flour
1 cup water
¾ cup sugar
1 teaspoon vanilla

1. Place bread cubes in greased crock pot. 2. Beat together eggs and milk. Stir in sugar, butter, raisins, and cinnamon. Pour over bread and stir. 3. Cover and cook on high 1 hour. Reduce heat to low and cook 3 to 4 hours, or until thermometer reaches 160°F (71°C). 4. Make sauce just before pudding is done baking. Begin by melting butter in saucepan. Stir in flour until smooth. Gradually add water, sugar, and vanilla. Bring to boil. Cook, stirring constantly for 2 minutes, or until thickened. 5. Serve sauce over warm bread pudding.

Cinnamon Pecans

Prep time: 15 minutes | Cook time: 3 to 4 hours | Makes about 3½ cups

1 tablespoon coconut oil
1 large egg white
2 tablespoons ground cinnamon
2 teaspoons vanilla extract

¼ cup maple syrup
2 tablespoons coconut sugar
¼ teaspoon sea salt
3 cups pecan halves

1. Coat the crock pot with the coconut oil. 2. In a medium bowl, whisk the egg white. 3. Add the cinnamon, vanilla, maple syrup, coconut sugar, and salt. Whisk well to combine. 4. Add the pecans and stir to coat. Pour the pecans into the crock pot. 5. Cover the cooker and set to low. Cook for 3 to 4 hours. 6. Remove the pecans from the crock pot and spread them on a baking sheet or other cooling surface. Let cool for 5 to 10 minutes before serving. Store in an airtight container at room temperature for up to 2 weeks.

Peanut Butter and Hot Fudge Pudding Cake

Prep time: 10 minutes | Cook time: 2 to 3 hours | Serves 6

½ cup flour	¼ cup peanut butter
¼ cup sugar	½ cup sugar
¾ teaspoon baking powder	3 tablespoons unsweetened
⅓ cup milk	cocoa powder
1 tablespoon oil	1 cup boiling water
½ teaspoon vanilla	Vanilla ice cream

1. Combine flour, ¼ cup sugar, and baking powder. Add milk, oil, and vanilla. Mix until smooth. Stir in peanut butter. Pour into crock pot. 2. Mix together ½ cup sugar and cocoa powder. 3. Gradually stir in boiling water. Pour mixture over batter in crock pot. Do not stir. Cover and cook on high 2 to 3 hours, or until toothpick inserted comes out clean. 4. Serve warm with ice cream.

Fruit Dessert Topping

Prep time: 20 minutes | Cook time: 3½ to 4¾ hours | Makes 6 cups

3 tart apples, peeled and sliced	½ cup chopped pecans
3 pears, peeled and sliced	¼ cup raisins
1 tablespoon lemon juice	2 cinnamon sticks
½ cup packed brown sugar	1 tablespoon cornstarch
½ cup maple syrup	2 tablespoons cold water
¼ cup butter, melted	

1. Toss apples and pears in lemon juice in crock pot. 2. Combine brown sugar, maple syrup, and butter. Pour over fruit. 3. Stir in pecans, raisins, and cinnamon sticks. 4. Cover. Cook on low 3 to 4 hours. 5. Combine cornstarch and water until smooth. Gradually stir into crock pot. 6. Cover. Cook on high 30 to 40 minutes, or until thickened. 7. Discard cinnamon sticks. Serve.

"Baked" Custard

Prep time: 10 minutes | Cook time: 2 to 3 hours | Serves 5 to 6

2 cups whole milk	divided
3 eggs, slightly beaten	1 teaspoon vanilla
⅓ cup plus ½ teaspoon sugar,	¼ teaspoon cinnamon

1. Heat milk in a small uncovered saucepan until a skin forms on top. Remove from heat and let cool slightly. 2. Meanwhile, in a large mixing bowl combine eggs, ⅓ cup sugar, and vanilla. 3. Slowly stir cooled milk into egg-sugar mixture. 4. Pour into a greased 1-quart baking dish which will fit into your crock pot, or into a baking insert designed for your crock pot. 5. Mix cinnamon and ½ teaspoon reserved sugar in a small bowl. Sprinkle over custard mixture. 6. Cover baking dish or insert with foil. Set container on a metal rack or trivet in crock pot. Pour hot water around dish to a depth of 1 inch. 7. Cover cooker. Cook on high 2 to 3 hours, or until custard is set. (When blade of a knife inserted in center of custard comes out clean, custard is set.) 8. Serve warm from baking dish or insert.

Zesty Pears

Prep time: 15 minutes | Cook time: 4 to 6 hours | Serves 6

6 fresh pears	¼ cup brandy
½ cup raisins	½ cup sauternes wine
¼ cup brown sugar	½ cup macaroon crumbs
1 teaspoon grated lemon peel	

1. Peel and core pears. Cut into thin slices. 2. Combine raisins, sugar, and lemon peel. Layer alternately with pear slices in crock pot. 3. Pour brandy and wine over top. 4. Cover. Cook on low 4 to 6 hours. 5. Spoon into serving dishes. Cool. Sprinkle with macaroons. Serve.

Upside-Down Chocolate Pudding Cake

Prep time: 15 minutes | Cook time: 2 to 3 hours | Serves 8

1 cup dry all-purpose baking mix	divided
	½ cup milk
1 cup sugar, divided	1 teaspoon vanilla
3 tablespoons unsweetened cocoa powder, plus ⅓ cup,	1⅔ cups hot water
	Nonstick cooking spray

1. Spray inside of crock pot with nonstick cooking spray. 2. In a bowl, mix together baking mix, ½ cup sugar, 3 tablespoons cocoa powder, milk, and vanilla. Spoon batter evenly into crock pot. 3. In a clean bowl, mix remaining ½ cup sugar, ⅓ cup cocoa powder, and hot water together. Pour over batter in crock pot. Do not stir. 4. Cover and cook on high 2 to 3 hours, or until toothpick inserted in center of cake comes out clean.

Apple Crisp

Prep time: 10 minutes | Cook time: 2 to 3 hours |
Serves 6 to 8

1 quart canned apple pie filling	½ cup flour
¾ cup quick oatmeal	¼ cup butter, at room
½ cup brown sugar	temperature

1. Place pie filling in crock pot. 2. Combine remaining ingredients until crumbly. Sprinkle over apple filling. 3. Cover. Cook on low 2 to 3 hours.

Apple Dish

Prep time: 20 minutes | Cook time: 2 to 2½ hours |
Makes about 7 cups

¾ cup sugar	cored, and diced into ¾-inch
3 tablespoons flour	pieces
1½ teaspoons cinnamon	Half a stick butter, melted
(optional)	3 tablespoons water
5 large baking apples, pared,	Nonstick cooking spray

1. Spray interior of crock pot with nonstick cooking spray. 2. In a large bowl, mix sugar and flour together, along with cinnamon if you wish. Set aside. 3. Mix apples, butter, and water together in crock pot. Gently stir in flour mixture until apples are well coated. 4. Cover and cook on high 1½ hours, and then on low 30 to 60 minutes, or until apples are done to your liking. 5. Serve.

Peach Brown Betty

Prep time: 20 minutes | Cook time: 6 hours | Serves 10

8 ripe peaches, peeled and cut	bread
into chunks	1½ cups whole-wheat bread
1 cup dried cranberries	crumbs
2 tablespoons freshly squeezed	⅓ cup coconut sugar
lemon juice	¼ teaspoon ground cardamom
3 tablespoons honey	⅓ cup melted coconut oil
3 cups cubed whole-wheat	

1. In a 6-quart crock pot, mix the peaches, dried cranberries, lemon juice, and honey. 2. In a large bowl, mix the bread cubes, bread crumbs, coconut sugar, and cardamom. Drizzle the melted coconut oil over all and toss to coat. 3. Sprinkle the bread mixture on the fruit in the crock pot. 4. Cover and cook on low for 5 to 6 hours, or until the fruit is bubbling and the topping is browned.

Dried Fruit

Prep time: 5 minutes | Cook time: 4 to 8 hours |
Serves 3 to 4

2 cups mixed dried fruit	¼ cup water

1. Place dried fruit in crock pot. Add water. 2. Cover. Cook on low 4 to 8 hours. 3. Serve warm.

Low-Fat Apple Cake

Prep time: 15 minutes | Cook time: 2½ to 3 hours |
Serves 8

1 cup flour	4 medium cooking apples,
¾ cup sugar	chopped
2 teaspoons baking powder	⅓ cup eggbeaters
1 teaspoon ground cinnamon	2 teaspoons vanilla
¼ teaspoon salt	

1. Combine flour, sugar, baking powder, cinnamon, and salt. 2. Add apples, stirring lightly to coat. 3. Combine eggbeaters and vanilla. Add to apple mixture. Stir until just moistened. Spoon into lightly greased crock pot. 4. Cover. Cook on high 2½ to 3 hours. 5. Serve warm.

Hot Fudge Cake

Prep time: 10 minutes | Cook time: 1½ to 1¾ hours |
Serves 8

1¾ cups brown sugar, divided	½ cup skim milk
1 cup flour	2 tablespoons butter, melted
3 tablespoons, plus ¼ cup,	½ teaspoon vanilla
unsweetened cocoa, divided	1¾ cups boiling water
1½ teaspoons baking powder	Nonfat cooking spray
½ teaspoon salt	

1. In a mixing bowl, mix together 1 cup brown sugar, flour, 3 tablespoons cocoa, baking powder, and salt. 2. Stir in milk, butter, and vanilla. 3. Pour into crock pot sprayed with nonfat cooking spray. 4. In a separate bowl, mix together ¾ cup brown sugar and ¼ cup cocoa. Sprinkle over batter in the crock pot. Do not stir. 5. Pour boiling water over mixture. Do not stir. 6. Cover. Cook on high 1½ to 1¾ hours, or until toothpick inserted into cake comes out clean.

Coconut-Vanilla Yogurt

Prep time: 15 minutes | Cook time: 1 to 2 hours | Makes about 3½ cups

3 (13½-ounce / 383-g) cans full-fat coconut milk
5 probiotic capsules (not pills)

1 teaspoon raw honey
½ teaspoon vanilla extract

1. Pour the coconut milk into the crock pot. 2. Cover the cooker and set to high. Cook for 1 to 2 hours, until the temperature of the milk reaches 180°F measured with a candy thermometer. 3. Turn off the crock pot and allow the temperature of the milk to come down close to 100°F. 4. Open the probiotic capsules and pour in the contents, along with the honey and vanilla. Stir well to combine. 5. Re-cover the crock pot, turn it off and unplug it, and wrap it in an insulating towel to keep warm overnight as it ferments. 6. Pour the yogurt into sterilized jars and refrigerate. The yogurt should thicken slightly in the refrigerator, where it will keep for up to 1 week.

Poppy's Carrot Cake

Prep time: 20 minutes | Cook time: 3 hours | Serves 6 to 8

Carrot Cake:
Nonstick cooking spray (optional)
1 tablespoon ground flaxseed
2½ tablespoons water
2¼ cups rolled oats, divided
1¾ teaspoons ground cinnamon
¾ teaspoon ground nutmeg
¾ teaspoon ground ginger
2 teaspoons baking powder
1 teaspoon baking soda
1 cup unsweetened plant-based milk
¾ cup raisins, divided

¼ cup unsweetened applesauce
⅓ cup date syrup or maple syrup (optional)
1 medium banana, peeled and broken into pieces
1 teaspoon vanilla extract
2 cups grated carrots
½ cup walnut pieces (optional)
Frosting:
¾ cup raw cashews
6 pitted Medjool dates, chopped
½ teaspoon ground ginger
⅓ to ½ cup water
2 tablespoons coconut cream

1. Prepare the crock pot by folding two long sheets of aluminum foil and placing them perpendicular to each other (crisscross) in the bottom of the crock pot to create "handles" that will come out over the top of the crock pot. Coat the inside of the crock pot and foil with cooking spray (if using) or line it with a crock pot liner. 2. Make the carrot cake: Make a flax egg in a small bowl by mixing together the flaxseed and the water. Set aside. 3. In a blender or food processor, combine 1¾ cups of oats, the cinnamon, nutmeg, ginger, baking powder, and baking soda. Blend until the oats are turned into a flour. Pour into a large bowl and set aside. Add the remaining ½ cup of whole oats to the dry ingredients. 4. Without

rinsing the blender or food processor, add the milk, ¼ cup of raisins, applesauce, syrup (if using), banana, vanilla, and the flax egg. Process until smooth and the raisins are broken down. Pour over the dry ingredients. Add the carrots, the remaining ½ cup of raisins, and the walnuts (if using), and stir well to combine. 5. Pour the mixture into the prepared crock pot. Stretch a clean dish towel or a few layers of paper towels over the top of the crock pot and cover. Cook on Low for 3 hours. The carrot cake is ready when a toothpick inserted in the center comes out clean. Remove the insert from the crock pot and cool on a wire rack for at least 30 minutes before removing the cake from the insert. Allow to cool completely before frosting. 6. Make the frosting: Put the cashews, dates, and ginger in a blender or food processor. Cover with just enough water to submerge the cashews and dates. Let the mixture soak for up to 1 hour to soften. Add the coconut cream and blend well until creamy. The frosting will thicken slightly as it sits.

Gooey Bittersweet Chocolate Pudding Cake

Prep time: 15 minutes | Cook time: 3 to 4 hours | Serves 6 to 8

Cake:
1 cup whole-wheat flour
¼ cup cocoa powder
2 teaspoons baking powder
½ teaspoon ground cinnamon
¼ teaspoon salt (optional)
⅓ cup unsweetened applesauce
2 teaspoons vanilla extract
⅔ cup unsweetened vanilla or plain plant-based milk
2 tablespoons date syrup or

maple syrup (optional)
Nonstick cooking spray (optional)
Pudding:
¼ cup cocoa powder
1 teaspoon instant coffee
½ cup date syrup or maple syrup (optional)
1 teaspoon vanilla extract
1 cup hot water

1. Make the cake: In a medium bowl, whisk together the flour, cocoa powder, baking powder, cinnamon, and salt (if using). 2. In a separate medium bowl, whisk together the applesauce, vanilla, milk, and date syrup (if using). Pour the applesauce mixture into the flour mixture and stir until just fully combined. Do not overmix. 3. Coat the inside of the crock pot with cooking spray (if using) or line it with a crock pot liner. Add the cake batter and spread it over the bottom of the crock pot. 4. Make the pudding: In a medium bowl, whisk together the cocoa powder, coffee, date syrup (if using), vanilla, and hot water. Pour over the cake ingredients in the crock pot. The mixture will be watery. 5. Cover and cook on Low for 3 to 4 hours. When it is ready to serve, the cake will look dry on top and will have achieved a pudding-like texture below the surface. Enjoy it immediately for best results.

Clean Eating Brownies

Prep time: 20 minutes | Cook time: 5 hours | Serves 12

1½ cups whole-wheat pastry flour	1 cup mashed ripe bananas (about 2 medium)
¾ cup unsweetened cocoa powder	1 cup mashed peeled ripe pears
1 teaspoon baking powder	½ cup coconut sugar
5 tablespoons melted coconut oil	½ cup honey
	4 eggs
	2 teaspoons vanilla extract

1. Tear off two long strips of heavy-duty foil and fold to make long thin strips. Place in a 6-quart crock pot to make an X. Then line the crock pot with parchment paper on top of the foil. 2. In a medium bowl, combine the whole-wheat pastry flour, cocoa powder, and baking powder and stir to mix. 3. In another medium bowl, combine the melted coconut oil, mashed bananas, mashed pears, coconut sugar, honey, eggs, and vanilla and mix well. 4. Stir the banana mixture into the flour mixture just until combined. 5. Spoon the batter into the crock pot onto the parchment paper. 6. Cover and cook on low for 4 to 5 hours or until a toothpick inserted near the center comes out with just a few moist crumbs attached to it. 7. Carefully remove the brownie, using the foil sling. Let cool, then remove the brownie from the parchment paper and cut into squares to serve.

"Here Comes Autumn" Apple Crisp

Prep time: 15 minutes | Cook time: 2 to 3 hours | Serves 4 to 6

Apple Base:	Topping:
6 apples (about 2 pounds / 907 g), any variety, cored and thinly sliced	¾ cup chopped pecans
	½ cup almond meal or almond flour
1 tablespoon lemon juice	½ cup rolled oats
2 tablespoons maple syrup (optional)	3 tablespoons maple syrup (optional)
1 teaspoon ground cinnamon	½ teaspoon ground cinnamon
½ teaspoon grated nutmeg	¼ teaspoon grated nutmeg

1. Make the apple base: Put the apples in the crock pot and sprinkle with the lemon juice, tossing well to coat the apples completely. Stir in the maple syrup (if using), cinnamon, and nutmeg until the syrup and spices cover every apple slice. Spread the apples out in an even layer. 2. Make the topping and cook: In a medium bowl, combine the pecans, almond meal or flour, oats, maple syrup (if using), cinnamon, and nutmeg. Mix well until crumbles form. Spoon the mixture evenly over the apples. 3. To keep the condensation that forms on the inside of the lid away from the topping, stretch a clean dish towel or several layers of paper towels across the top of the crock pot, but not touching the food, and place the lid on top of the towel(s). If you skip this step, you will have a soggy result rather than a crunchy crumble. 4. Cook on High for 2 to 3 hours or on Low for 4 to 5 hours, until the apples are soft and cooked through.

Chai Spice Baked Apples

Prep time: 15 minutes | Cook time: 2 to 3 hours | Makes 5 apples

5 apples	1 teaspoon ground cinnamon
½ cup water	½ teaspoon ground ginger
½ cup crushed pecans (optional)	¼ teaspoon ground cardamom
¼ cup melted coconut oil	¼ teaspoon ground cloves

1. Core each apple, and peel off a thin strip from the top of each. 2. Add the water to the crock pot. Gently place each apple upright along the bottom. 3. In a small bowl, stir together the pecans (if using), coconut oil, cinnamon, ginger, cardamom, and cloves. Drizzle the mixture over the tops of the apples. 4. Cover the cooker and set to high. Cook for 2 to 3 hours, until the apples soften, and serve.

Apple-Granola Bake

Prep time: 10 minutes | Cook time: 6 to 8 hours | Serves 6

Nonstick cooking spray	2 cups almond milk
2 cups steel-cut oats	¼ cup honey or maple syrup
2 apples, finely diced, divided	1 ripe banana, mashed
⅓ cup semisweet chocolate chips, divided	1 large egg
1 teaspoon baking powder	1 tablespoon pure vanilla extract
1 teaspoon ground cinnamon	1 banana, cut into ½-inch slices
½ teaspoon salt	

1. Spray the crock pot generously with nonstick cooking spray. 2. In a large bowl, mix together the oats, 1 of the diced apples, about half of the chocolate chips, and the baking powder, cinnamon, and salt. 3. In a separate large bowl, whisk together the almond milk, honey, mashed banana, egg, and vanilla. The honey might clump up at first; just keep whisking. 4. Pour the oat mixture into the crock pot. Add the remaining apple and chocolate chips, and spread the banana slices on top. 5. Pour the honey mixture on top of everything. Gently shake the crock pot to make sure all of the dry mixture is completely wet. 6. Cook on low for 6 to 8 hours, or until the oatmeal is set, and serve. (You'll know it's done when you insert a knife and it comes out clean.)

Spiced Apples

Prep time: 5 minutes | Cook time: 4 to 5 hours | Serves 10 to 12

16 cups sliced apples, peeled or unpeeled, divided
½ cup brown sugar, divided
3 tablespoons minute tapioca,
divided
1 teaspoon ground cinnamon,
divided

1. Layer half of sliced apples, sugar, tapioca, and cinnamon in crock pot. 2. Repeat, making a second layer using remaining ingredients. 3. Cover. Cook on high 4 hours, or on low 5 hours. 4. Stir before serving.

Fruited Rice Pudding

Prep time: 20 minutes | Cook time: 6 hours | Serves 16

6 cups canned coconut milk
3 cups water
1⅔ cups brown Arborio rice
½ cup coconut sugar
2 tablespoons coconut oil
1 cup raisins
1 tablespoon vanilla extract
1 cup dark chocolate chips
(optional)

1. In a 6-quart crock pot, mix the coconut milk and water. Add the rice and coconut sugar and mix. Add the coconut oil and the raisins. 2. Cover and cook on low for 5 to 6 hours, or until the rice is very tender. 3. Stir in the vanilla. If using, serve the pudding with the chocolate chips sprinkled on top.

Peach Cobbler

Prep time: 15 minutes | Cook time: 1 to 2 hours | Serves 6 to 8

Filling:
2 (15-ounce / 425-g) cans
peaches in juice
½ teaspoon ground cinnamon
½ teaspoon ground ginger
3 tablespoons maple syrup or
date syrup (optional)
2 tablespoons cornstarch

Topping:
1 cup rolled oats
¼ teaspoon ground cinnamon
2 tablespoons coconut cream
1 tablespoon liquid from the
canned peaches
4 tablespoons date syrup
(optional)

1. Make the filling: Remove the peaches from the cans, reserving the juice. Slice the peaches into bite-size chunks and put them in the crock pot. Stir in the cinnamon, ginger, syrup (if using), and cornstarch. 2. Make the topping and cook: In a medium bowl, combine the oats, cinnamon, coconut cream, canned peach liquid, and date syrup (if using). Stir together until the oats are wet and crumbly. Sprinkle over the peaches in the crock pot. 3. To keep the condensation that forms on the inside of the lid away from the topping, stretch a clean dish towel or several layers of paper towels over the top of the crock pot, but not touching the food, and place the lid on top of the towel(s). If you skip this step, you will have a soggy result. Cook on High for 1 to 2 hours or on Low for 2 to 3 hours.

Apple-Peach Crumble

Prep time: 20 minutes | Cook time: 5 hours | Serves 8

6 large Granny Smith apples,
peeled and cut into chunks
4 large peaches, peeled and
sliced
3 tablespoons honey
2 tablespoons lemon juice
1 cup almond flour
1 teaspoon ground cinnamon
3 cups quick-cooking oatmeal
⅓ cup coconut sugar
½ cup slivered almonds
½ cup melted coconut oil

1. In a 6-quart crock pot, mix the apples, peaches, honey, and lemon juice. 2. In a large bowl, mix the almond flour, cinnamon, oatmeal, coconut sugar, and almonds until well combined. 3. Add the coconut oil and mix until crumbly. 4. Sprinkle the almond mixture over the fruit in the crock pot. 5. Cover and cook on low for 4 to 5 hours, or until the fruit is tender and the crumble is bubbling around the edges.

Berry Crisp

Prep time: 20 minutes | Cook time: 6 hours | Serves 12

3 cups frozen organic
blueberries
3 cups frozen organic
raspberries
3 cups frozen organic
strawberries
2 tablespoons lemon juice
2½ cups rolled oats
1 cup whole-wheat flour
⅓ cup maple sugar
1 teaspoon ground cinnamon
⅓ cup coconut melted oil

1. Do not thaw the berries. In a 6-quart crock pot, mix the frozen berries. Drizzle with the lemon juice. 2. In a large bowl, mix the oats, flour, maple sugar, and cinnamon until well combined. Stir in the melted coconut oil until crumbly. 3. Sprinkle the oat mixture over the fruit in the crock pot. 4. Cover and cook on low for 5 to 6 hours, or until the fruit is bubbling and the topping is browned.

Chocolate's Best Friends Brownies

Prep time: 15 minutes | Cook time: 3½ hours | Makes about 2 dozen brownies

1¼ cups oats

¾ cup white beans, drained, and rinsed

¾ cup plus 3 tablespoons maple syrup (optional)

¼ cup plus 2 tablespoons unsweetened applesauce

1½ teaspoons vanilla extract

1½ teaspoons baking powder

½ teaspoon salt (optional)

¾ cup unsweetened cocoa powder

½ teaspoon ground cinnamon

1 teaspoon instant coffee

1. Crumple two pieces of aluminum foil to form a ring around the interior base of the crock pot. Add a liner or piece of parchment and set the crock pot to Low to preheat. 2. Put the oats in a blender or food processor and process into oat flour. Pour it into a small bowl and set aside. 3. Add the beans, maple syrup (if using), applesauce, and vanilla to the blender and blend until well combined, about 1 minute. Add the oat flour, baking powder, salt (if using), cocoa powder, cinnamon, and instant coffee. Blend until smooth and thick, scraping down the sides as needed. 4. Spread the batter into the prepared crock pot. Cover and cook on Low for 3½ hours. Turn off the crock pot, remove the cover, and let the brownies cool completely before slicing, at least 1 hour. Store at room temperature for 2 to 3 days.

Creamy Dreamy Brown Rice Pudding

Prep time: 5 minutes | Cook time: 2 to 3 hours | Serves 6 to 8

Nonstick cooking spray (optional)

1 cup brown rice

4 cups unsweetened vanilla plant-based milk

¼ cup maple syrup or date syrup (optional)

2 teaspoons ground cinnamon

2 teaspoons vanilla extract

½ cup raisins, for topping (optional)

1.Coat the inside of the crock pot with cooking spray (if using) or line it with a crock pot liner. 2. Add the rice, milk, syrup (if using), cinnamon, and vanilla, and stir to combine. 3. Cover and cook on High for 2 to 3 hours or on Low for 3 to 4 hours, stirring when there is an hour left to check for doneness and your preference for the rice. Cook it longer for creamier pudding or shorter for a more toothsome texture. Just before serving, top with the raisins (if using) for extra sweetness and texture.

Chapter 9 Stews and Soups

Creamy Corn and Turkey Soup

Prep time: 15 minutes | Cook time: 3 to 8 hours | Serves 5 to 6

2 cups cooked turkey, shredded
1 cup milk
2 cups chicken broth
1 (15-ounce / 425-g) can
Mexican-style corn

4 ounces (113 g) cream cheese,
cubed
1 red bell pepper, chopped
(optional)

1. Place all ingredients in crock pot. 2. Cover and cook on low 7 to 8 hours, or on high 3 hours.

Caribbean-Style Black Bean Soup

Prep time: 10 minutes | Cook time: 4 to 10 hours | Serves 8 to 10

1 pound (454 g) dried black
beans, washed and stones
removed
3 onions, chopped
1 green pepper, chopped
4 coves garlic, minced
1 ham hock, or ¾ cup cubed
ham
1 tablespoon oil

1 tablespoon ground cumin
2 teaspoons dried oregano
1 teaspoon dried thyme
1 tablespoon salt
½ teaspoon pepper
3 cups water
2 tablespoons vinegar
Sour cream
Fresh chopped cilantro

1. Soak beans overnight in 4 quarts water. Drain. 2. Combine beans, onions, green pepper, garlic, ham, oil, cumin, oregano, thyme, salt, pepper, and 3 cups fresh water. Stir well. 3. Cover. Cook on low 8 to 10 hours, or on high 4 to 5 hours. 4. For a thick soup, remove half of cooked bean mixture and purée until smooth in blender or mash with potato masher. Return to cooker. If you like a thinner soup, leave as is. 5. Add vinegar and stir well. Debone ham, cut into bite-sized pieces, and return to soup. 6. Serve in soup bowls with a dollop of sour cream in the middle of each individual serving, topped with fresh cilantro.

Chili, Chicken, Corn Chowder

Prep time: 15 minutes | Cook time: 4 hours | Serves 6 to 8

¼ cup oil
1 large onion, diced
1 garlic clove, minced
1 rib celery, finely chopped
2 cups frozen or canned corn
2 cups cooked chicken, deboned
and cubed

1 (4-ounce / 113-g) can diced
green chilies
½ teaspoon black pepper
2 cups chicken broth
Salt to taste
1 cup half-and-half

1. In saucepan, sauté onion, garlic, and celery in oil until limp. 2. Stir in corn, chicken, and chilies. Sauté for 2 to 3 minutes. 3. Combine all ingredients except half-and-half in crock pot. 4. Cover. Heat on low 4 hours. 5. Stir in half-and-half before serving. Do not boil, but be sure cream is heated through.

Turkey Rosemary Veggie Soup

Prep time: 15 minutes | Cook time: 8 hours | Serves 8

1 pound (454 g) 99% fat-free
ground turkey
3 parsley stalks with leaves,
sliced
3 scallions, chopped
3 medium carrots, unpeeled,
sliced
3 medium potatoes, unpeeled,
sliced
3 celery ribs with leaves
3 small onions, sliced
1 (1-pound / 454-g) can whole-

kernel corn with juice
1 (1-pound / 454-g) can green
beans with juice
1 (1-pound / 454-g) can low-
sodium diced Italian-style
tomatoes
3 cans water
3 packets dry Herb-Ox
vegetable broth
1 tablespoon crushed rosemary,
fresh or dry

1. Brown turkey with parsley and scallions in iron skillet. Drain. Pour into crock pot sprayed with nonfat cooking spray. 2. Add vegetables, water, dry vegetable broth, and rosemary. 3. Cover. Cook on low 8 hours.

Split Pea Soup with Ham

Prep time: 15 minutes | Cook time: 4 hours | Serves 8

2½ quarts water
1 ham hock or pieces of cut-up ham
2½ cups split peas, dried

1 medium onion, chopped
3 medium carrots, cut in small pieces
Salt and pepper to taste

1. Bring water to a boil in a saucepan on your stovetop. 2. Place all other ingredients into crock pot. Add water and stir together well. 3. Cover and cook on high for 4 hours, or until vegetables are tender. 4. If you've cooked a ham hock, remove it from the soup and debone the meat. Stir cut-up chunks of meat back into the soup before serving.

Taco Soup with Pizza Sauce

Prep time: 15 minutes | Cook time: 3 to 4 hours | Serves 8 to 10

2 pounds (907 g) ground beef, browned
1 small onion, chopped and sautéed in ground beef drippings
¾ teaspoon salt
½ teaspoon pepper

1½ packages dry taco seasoning
1 quart pizza sauce
1 quart water
Tortilla chips
Shredded Mozzarella cheese
Sour cream

1. Combine ground beef, onion, salt, pepper, taco seasoning, pizza sauce, and water in 5-quart, or larger, crock pot. 2. Cover. Cook on low 3 to 4 hours. 3. Top individual servings with tortilla chips, cheese, and sour cream.

Bratwurst Stew

Prep time: 15 minutes | Cook time: 3 to 4 hours | Serves 8

2 (10¾-ounce / 305-g) cans fat-free chicken broth
4 medium carrots, sliced
2 ribs of celery, cut in chunks
1 medium onion, chopped
1 teaspoon dried basil

½ teaspoon garlic powder
3 cups chopped cabbage
2 (1-pound / 454-g) cans Great Northern beans, drained
5 fully cooked bratwurst links, cut into ½-inch slices

1. Combine all ingredients in crock pot. 2. Cook on high 3 to 4 hours, or until veggies are tender.

Clam Chowder

Prep time: 10 minutes | Cook time: 2 to 3 hours | Serves 3

1 (15-ounce / 425-g) can New England-style clam chowder
1½ cups milk or half-and-half
1 (6½-ounce / 184-g) can

minced clams, undrained
Half a stick (¼ cup) butter
¼ cup cooking sherry

1. Mix all ingredients together in crock pot. 2. Heat on low for 2 to 3 hours, or until good and hot.

No-Fuss Potato Soup

Prep time: 15 minutes | Cook time: 7 to 8 hours | Serves 8 to 10

6 cups diced, peeled potatoes
5 cups water
2 cups diced onions
½ cup diced celery
½ cup chopped carrots
¼ cup butter
4 teaspoons chicken bouillon granules

2 teaspoons salt
¼ teaspoon pepper
1 (12-ounce / 340-g) can evaporated milk
3 tablespoons chopped fresh parsley
8 ounces (227 g) Cheddar, or Colby, cheese, shredded

1. Combine all ingredients except milk, parsley, and cheese in crock pot. 2. Cover. Cook on high 7 to 8 hours, or until vegetables are tender. 3. Stir in milk and parsley. Stir in cheese until it melts. Heat thoroughly.

Lotsa-Tomatoes Beef Stew

Prep time: 15 minutes | Cook time: 5½ to 6 hours | Serves 6

2 pounds (907 g) extra-lean stewing beef cubes, trimmed of fat
5 to 6 carrots, cut in 1-inch pieces
1 large onion, cut in chunks
3 ribs celery, sliced
6 medium tomatoes, cut up and gently mashed

½ cup quick-cooking tapioca
1 whole clove, or ¼ to ½ teaspoon ground cloves
1 teaspoon dried basil
½ teaspoon dried oregano
2 bay leaves
2 teaspoons salt
½ teaspoon black pepper
3 to 4 potatoes, cubed

1. Place all ingredients in crock pot. Mix together well. 2. Cover. Cook on high 5½ to 6 hours.

Tasty Chicken Soup

Prep time: 15 minutes | Cook time: 6 to 7 hours | Serves 12

12 cups chicken broth	Small onion
2 cups cooked chicken, cubed	1 (16-ounce / 454-g) bag of dry
1 cup shredded carrots	noodles, cooked (optional)
3 whole cloves	

1. Place broth, chicken, and carrots in crock pot. 2. Peel onion. Using a toothpick, poke 3 holes on the cut ends. Carefully press cloves into 3 of the holes until only their round part shows. Add to crock pot. 3. Cover and cook on high 6 to 7 hours. 4. If you'd like a thicker soup, add a bag of cooked fine egg noodles before serving.

Sauerkraut Potato Soup

Prep time: 15 minutes | Cook time: 2 to 8 hours | Serves 8

1 pound (454 g) smoked Polish sausage, cut into ½-inch pieces	1 (42-ounce / 1.2-kg) can chicken broth
5 medium potatoes, cubed	1 (32-ounce / 907-g) can or bag
2 large onions, chopped	sauerkraut, rinsed and drained
2 large carrots, cut into ¼-inch slices	1 (6-ounce / 170-g) can tomato paste

1. Combine all ingredients in large crock pot. Stir to combine. 2. Cover. Cook on high 2 hours, and then on low 6 to 8 hours. 3. Serve.

Vegetarian Chili Soup

Prep time: 10 minutes | Cook time: 4 to 9½ hours | Serves 8

1 large onion, chopped	tomatoes
1 tablespoon margarine	5 cups water
1 clove garlic, finely chopped	½ teaspoon salt
2 teaspoons chili powder	¼ teaspoon black pepper
½ teaspoon dried oregano, crumbled	¾ pound (340 g) fresh kale
2 (14½-ounce / 411-g) cans vegetable broth	⅓ cup white long-grain rice
1 (14½-ounce / 411-g) can no-salt-added stewed or diced	1 (19-ounce / 539-g) can cannellini beans, drained and rinsed

1. Sauté onion in skillet with margarine until tender. 2. Add garlic, chili powder, and oregano. Cook for 30 seconds. Pour into crock pot. 3. Add remaining ingredients except kale, rice, and beans. 4. Cover. Cook on low 7 hours, or on high 3 to 4 hours. 5. Cut kale stalks into small pieces and chop leaves coarsely. 6. Add to soup with rice and beans. 7. Cover. Cook on high 1 to 2½ hours more, or until rice is tender and kale is done to your liking.

Vegetable Salmon Chowder

Prep time: 15 minutes | Cook time: 3 hours | Serves 8

1½ cups cubed potatoes	salmon
1 cup diced celery	4 cups skim milk
½ cup diced onions	2 teaspoons lemon juice
2 tablespoons fresh parsley, or	2 tablespoons finely cut red bell
1 tablespoon dried parsley	peppers
½ teaspoon salt	2 tablespoons finely shredded
¼ teaspoon black pepper	carrots
Water to cover	½ cup instant potatoes
1 (16-ounce / 454-g) can pink	

1. Combine cubed potatoes, celery, onions, parsley, salt, pepper, and water to cover in crock pot. 2. Cook on high for 3 hours, or until soft. Add a bit more water if needed. 3. Add salmon, milk, lemon juice, red peppers, carrots, and instant potatoes. 4. Heat 1 hour more until very hot.

Lentil-Tomato Stew

Prep time: 10 minutes | Cook time: 4 to 12 hours | Serves 8

3 cups water	rinsed and drained with any
1 (28-ounce / 794-g) can low-sodium peeled Italian tomatoes, undrained	stones removed
	1 large onion, chopped
1 (6-ounce / 170-g) can low-sodium tomato paste	4 medium carrots, cut in ½-inch rounds
½ cup dry red wine	4 medium celery ribs, cut into
¾ teaspoon dried basil	½-inch slices
¾ teaspoon dried thyme	3 garlic cloves, minced
½ teaspoon crushed red pepper	1 teaspoon salt
1 pound (454 g) dried lentils,	Chopped fresh basil or parsley, for garnish

1. Combine water, tomatoes with juice, tomato paste, red wine, basil, thyme, and crushed red pepper in crock pot. 2. Break up tomatoes with a wooden spoon and stir to blend them and the paste into the mixture. 3. Add lentils, onion, carrots, celery, and garlic. 4. Cover. Cook on low 10 to 12 hours, or on high 4 to 5 hours. 5. Stir in the salt. 6. Serve in bowls, sprinkled with chopped basil or parsley.

Tomato Green Bean Soup

Prep time: 10 minutes | Cook time: 6 to 8 hours | Serves 8

1 cup chopped onions
1 cup chopped carrots
6 cups low-fat, reduced-sodium chicken broth
1 pound (454 g) fresh green beans, cut in 1-inch pieces

1 clove garlic, minced
3 cups fresh, diced tomatoes
1 teaspoon dried basil
½ teaspoon salt
¼ teaspoon black pepper

1. Combine all ingredients in crock pot. 2. Cover. Cook on low 6 to 8 hours.

Lazy Day Stew

Prep time: 15 minutes | Cook time: 8 hours | Serves 8

2 pounds (907 g) stewing beef, cubed
2 cups diced carrots
2 cups diced potatoes
2 medium onions, chopped
1 cup chopped celery
1 (10-ounce / 283-g) package lima beans

2 teaspoons quick-cooking tapioca
1 teaspoon salt
½ teaspoon pepper
1 (8-ounce / 227-g) can tomato sauce
1 cup water
1 tablespoon brown sugar

1. Place beef in bottom of crock pot. Add vegetables. 2. Sprinkle tapioca, salt, and pepper over ingredients. 3. Mix together tomato sauce and water. Pour over top. 4. Sprinkle brown sugar over all. 5. Cover. Cook on low 8 hours.

Vegetable Cheese Soup

Prep time: 15 minutes | Cook time: 4 to 10 hours | Serves 5

2 cups cream-style corn
1 cup peeled and chopped potatoes
1 cup peeled and chopped carrots

2 (14½-ounce / 411-g) cans vegetable or chicken broth
1 (16-ounce / 454-g) jar processed cheese

1. Combine all ingredients except cheese in the crock pot. 2. Cover and cook on low 8 to 10 hours, or on high 4 to 5 hours. 3. Thirty to 60 minutes before serving, stir in the cheese. Then cook on high for 30 to 60 minutes to melt and blend the cheese.

Taco Soup with Hominy

Prep time: 15 minutes | Cook time: 4 hours | Serves 8

1 pound (454 g) ground beef
1 envelope dry ranch dressing mix
1 envelope dry taco seasoning mix
3 (12-ounce / 340-g) cans Rotel tomatoes, undrained
2 (24-ounce / 680-g) cans pinto

beans, undrained
1 (24-ounce / 680-g) can hominy, undrained
1 (14½-ounce / 411-g) can stewed tomatoes, undrained
1 onion, chopped
2 cups water

1. Brown meat in skillet. Pour into crock pot. 2. Add remaining ingredients. Mix well. 3. Cover. Cook on low 4 hours.

"Mom's Favorite" Vegetable Soup

Prep time: 10 minutes | Cook time: 6 to 8 hours | Serves 5

½ cup dry pearl barley
1 (14½-ounce / 411-g) can low-sodium diced tomatoes
1 cup frozen corn
1 cup frozen peas
4 carrots, peeled and sliced
1 cup frozen green beans
Water to cover
5 cubes low-sodium beef

bouillon
5 cubes low-sodium chicken bouillon
½ teaspoon salt
½ teaspoon black pepper
½ teaspoon dried basil
1 teaspoon fresh thyme
½ teaspoon fresh dill
1 teaspoon fresh parsley

1. Combine all ingredients in crock pot, except fresh herbs. 2. Cover. Cook on low 6 to 8 hours. 3. Just before serving, stir in fresh thyme, dill, and parsley.

Mountain Bike Soup

Prep time: 10 minutes | Cook time: 2 to 6 hours | Serves 4

1 (12-ounce / 340-g) can chicken broth
1 (12-ounce / 340-g) can V-8 juice, regular or spicy
⅓ cup barley, rice, or broken

spaghetti noodles, uncooked
⅓ cup chopped pepperoni, ham, or bacon
1 (15-ounce / 425-g) can cut green beans with liquid

1. Dump it all in. Put on the lid. Turn it on low. 2. Go for a long ride on your bike, from 2 to 6 hours.

Tempting Beef Stew

Prep time: 10 minutes | Cook time: 10 to 12 hours |
Serves 10 to 12

2 to 3 pounds (907 g to 1.4 kg) beef stewing meat
3 carrots, thinly sliced
1 (1-pound / 454-g) package frozen green peas with onions
1 (1-pound / 454-g) package frozen green beans
1 (16-ounce / 454-g) can whole or stewed tomatoes
½ cup beef broth
½ cup white wine
½ cup brown sugar
4 tablespoons tapioca
½ cup bread crumbs
2 teaspoons salt
1 bay leaf
Pepper to taste

1. Combine all ingredients in crock pot. 2. Cover. Cook on low 10 to 12 hours. 3. Serve.

Vegetable Beef Soup

Prep time: 15 minutes | Cook time: 4 to 6 hours |
Serves 8

1 pound (454 g) extra-lean ground beef
1 (14½-ounce / 411-g) can low-sodium, stewed tomatoes
1 (10¾-ounce / 305-g) can low-sodium tomato soup
1 onion, chopped
2 cups water
1 (15½-ounce / 439-g) can garbanzo beans, drained
1 (15¼-ounce / 432-g) can corn, drained
1 (14½-ounce / 411-g) can sliced carrots, drained
1 cup diced potatoes
1 cup chopped celery
½ teaspoon salt
¼ teaspoon black pepper
Chopped garlic to taste (optional)

1. Sauté ground beef in nonstick skillet. 2. Combine all ingredients in crock pot. 3. Cook on low 4 to 6 hours.

Chicken Rice and Veggies Soup

Prep time: 30 minutes | Cook time: 4 to 8 hours |
Serves 8

4 cups chicken broth
4 cups cooked chicken, cubed or shredded
1⅓ cups cut-up celery
1⅓ cups diced carrots
1 quart water
1 cup long-grain rice, uncooked

1. Put all ingredients in crock pot. 2. Cover and cook on low 4 to 8 hours, or until vegetables are cooked to your liking.

Quick Clam and Corn Chowder

Prep time: 10 minutes | Cook time: 3 to 4 hours |
Serves 4 to 6

2 (10½-ounce / 298-g) cans cream of potato soup
1 pint frozen corn
1 (6½-ounce / 184-g) can minced clams, drained
2 soup cans milk

1. Place all ingredients in crock pot. Stir to mix. 2. Cook on low 3 to 4 hours, or until hot.

Onion Soup

Prep time: 30 minutes | Cook time: 6 to 8 hours |
Serves 8

3 medium onions, thinly sliced
2 tablespoons butter
2 tablespoons vegetable oil
1 teaspoon salt
1 tablespoon sugar
2 tablespoons flour
1 quart fat-free, low-sodium vegetable broth
½ cup dry white wine
Slices of French bread
½ cup grated fat-free Swiss or Parmesan cheese

1. Sauté onions in butter and oil in covered skillet until soft. Uncover. Add salt and sugar. Cook 15 minutes. Stir in flour. Cook 3 more minutes. 2. Combine onions, broth, and wine in crock pot. 3. Cover. Cook on low 6 to 8 hours. 4. Toast bread. Sprinkle with grated cheese and then broil. 5. Dish soup into individual bowls; then float a slice of broiled bread on top of each serving of soup.

French Market Soup

Prep time: 10 minutes | Cook time: 10 hours |
Serves 8

2 cups dry bean mix, washed with stones removed
2 quarts water
1 ham hock
1 teaspoon salt
¼ teaspoon pepper
1 (16-ounce / 454-g) can
tomatoes
1 large onion, chopped
1 garlic clove, minced
1 chili pepper, chopped, or 1 teaspoon chili powder
¼ cup lemon juice

1. Combine all ingredients in crock pot. 2. Cover. Cook on low 8 hours. Turn to high and cook an additional 2 hours, or until beans are tender. 3. Debone ham, cut meat into bite-sized pieces, and stir back into soup.

Grace's Minestrone Soup

Prep time: 15 minutes | Cook time: 8 hours | Serves 8

¾ cup dry elbow macaroni

2 quarts chicken stock

2 large onions, diced

2 carrots, sliced

Half a head of cabbage, shredded

½ cup diced celery

1 (1-pound / 454-g) can tomatoes

½ teaspoon salt

½ teaspoon dried oregano

1 tablespoon minced parsley

¼ cup each frozen corn, peas, and lima beans

¼ teaspoon pepper

Grated Parmesan or Romano cheese

1. Cook macaroni according to package directions. Set aside. 2. Combine all ingredients except macaroni and cheese in large crock pot. 3. Cover. Cook on low 8 hours. Add macaroni during last 30 minutes of cooking time. 4. Garnish individual servings with cheese.

Joy's Brunswick Stew

Prep time: 10 minutes | Cook time: 4 hours | Serves 8

1 pound (454 g) skinless, boneless chicken breasts, cubed

2 potatoes, thinly sliced

1 (10¾-ounce / 305-g) can tomato soup

1 (16-ounce / 454-g) can stewed tomatoes

1 (10-ounce / 283-g) package frozen corn

1 (10-ounce / 283-g) package frozen lima beans

3 tablespoons onion flakes

¼ teaspoon salt

⅛ teaspoon pepper

1. Combine all ingredients in crock pot. 2. Cover. Cook on high 2 hours. Reduce to low and cook 2 hours.

Curried Pork and Pea Soup

Prep time: 15 minutes | Cook time: 4 to 12 hours | Serves 6 to 8

1 (1½-pound / 680-g) boneless pork shoulder roast

1 cup yellow or green split peas, rinsed and drained

½ cup finely chopped carrots

½ cup finely chopped celery

½ cup finely chopped onions

6 cups chicken broth

2 teaspoons curry powder

½ teaspoon paprika

¼ teaspoon ground cumin

¼ teaspoon pepper

2 cups torn fresh spinach

1. Trim fat from pork and cut pork into ½-inch pieces. 2. Combine split peas, carrots, celery, and onions in crock pot. 3. Stir in broth, curry powder, paprika, cumin, and pepper. Stir in pork. 4. Cover. Cook on low 10 to 12 hours, or on high 4 hours. 5. Stir in spinach. Serve immediately.

Hamburger-Sausage Soup

Prep time: 25 minutes | Cook time: 8 to 10 hours | Serves 4 to 6

1 pound (454 g) ground beef

1 pound (454 g) Polish sausage, sliced

½ teaspoon seasoned salt

¼ teaspoon dried oregano

¼ teaspoon dried basil

1 package dry onion soup mix

6 cups boiling water

1 (16-ounce / 454-g) can diced tomatoes

1 tablespoon soy sauce

½ cup sliced celery

¼ cup chopped celery leaves

1 cup pared, sliced carrots

1 cup macaroni, uncooked

1. Brown ground beef and sausage in skillet. Drain. Place in crock pot. 2. Add seasoned salt, oregano, basil, and onion soup mix to cooker. 3. Stir in boiling water, tomatoes, and soy sauce. 4. Add celery, celery leaves, and carrots. Stir well. 5. Cover. Cook on low 8 to 10 hours. 6. One hour before end of cooking time, stir in dry macaroni. 7. Serve.

Minestrone

Prep time: 20 minutes | Cook time: 4 to 9 hours | Serves 8 to 10

1 large onion, chopped

4 carrots, sliced

3 ribs celery, sliced

2 garlic cloves, minced

1 tablespoon olive oil

1 (6-ounce / 170-g) can tomato paste

1 (14½-ounce / 411-g) can chicken, beef, or vegetable broth

1 (24-ounce / 680-g) can pinto beans, undrained

1 (10-ounce / 283-g) package

frozen green beans

2 to 3 cups chopped cabbage

1 medium zucchini, sliced

8 cups water

2 tablespoons parsley

2 tablespoons Italian spice

1 teaspoon salt, or more

½ teaspoon pepper

¾ cup dry acini di pepe (small round pasta)

Grated Parmesan or Asiago cheese

1. Sauté onion, carrots, celery, and garlic in oil until tender. 2. Combine all ingredients except pasta and cheese in crock pot. 3. Cover. Cook 4 to 5 hours on high or 8 to 9 hours on low, adding pasta 1 hour before cooking is complete. 4. Top individual servings with cheese.

Chet's Trucker Stew

Prep time: 15 minutes | Cook time: 2 to 3 hours | Serves 8

1 pound (454 g) bulk pork sausage, cooked and drained	kidney beans
1 pound (454 g) ground beef, cooked and drained	1 (14½-ounce / 411-g) can waxed beans, drained
1 (31-ounce / 879-g) can pork and beans	1 (14½-ounce / 411-g) can lima beans, drained
1 (16-ounce / 454-g) can light kidney beans	1 cup ketchup
	1 cup brown sugar
1 (16-ounce / 454-g) can dark	1 tablespoon spicy prepared mustard

1. Combine all ingredients in crock pot. 2. Cover. Simmer on high 2 to 3 hours.

Hungarian Barley Stew

Prep time: 20 minutes | Cook time: 5 hours | Serves 8

2 tablespoons oil	⅔ cup dry small pearl barley
1½ pounds (680 g) beef cubes	1 teaspoon salt
2 large onions, diced	½ teaspoon pepper
1 medium green pepper, chopped	1 tablespoon paprika
1 (28-ounce / 794-g) can whole tomatoes	1 (10-ounce / 283-g) package frozen baby lima beans
½ cup ketchup	3 cups water
	1 cup sour cream

1. Brown beef cubes in oil in skillet. Add onions and green peppers. Sauté. Pour into crock pot. 2. Add remaining ingredients except sour cream. 3. Cover. Cook on high 5 hours. 4. Stir in sour cream before serving. 5. Serve.

Bean and Bacon Soup

Prep time: 25 minutes | Cook time: 11 to 13½ hours | Serves 6

1¼ cups dried bean soup mix, or any combination of mixed dried beans	4 slices fried bacon (precooked bacon works well), crumbled
5 cups water	1 envelope taco seasoning
1 onion, chopped	2 (14-ounce / 397-g) cans diced tomatoes, undrained
3 cups water	

1. Place dried beans in large stockpot. Cover with 5 cups water. Cover pot and bring to a boil. Cook 2 minutes over high heat. 2.

Remove pot from heat and allow to stand, covered, for 1 hour. Return pot to stovetop and cook covered for 2½ to 3 hours, or until beans are tender. Drain. 3. Combine cooked beans, onion, 3 cups water, bacon, and taco seasoning in crock pot. Mix well. 4. Cook on low 8 to 10 hours. 5. Add tomatoes. Stir well. Cook another 30 minutes.

Vegetarian Soup

Prep time: 10 minutes | Cook time: 4 to 5 hours | Serves 6

1 (16-ounce / 454-g) can low-sodium diced tomatoes	½ cup low-sodium picante sauce
2 (15-ounce / 425-g) cans kidney or pinto beans, drained, divided	½ cup water
	½ teaspoon salt
1 cup chopped onions	1 teaspoon ground cumin
1 clove garlic, minced	1 teaspoon dried oregano
1 (8¾-ounce / 248-g) can whole-kernel corn, drained	1 green bell pepper, diced
	Reduced-fat shredded Cheddar cheese (optional)

1. Drain tomatoes, reserving juice. 2. Combine juice and 1 can beans in food processor bowl. Process until fairly smooth. 3. Combine all ingredients except green peppers and cheese in crock pot. 4. Cover. Cook on high 4 to 5 hours. 5. During last half hour add green peppers. 6. Ladle into bowls to serve. Top with cheese, if desired.

Taco Soup Plus

Prep time: 15 minutes | Cook time: 6 to 8 hours | Serves 6

Soup:	Toppings:
1 pound (454 g) extra-lean ground beef or ground turkey	¾ cup shredded lettuce
1 medium onion, chopped	6 tablespoons fresh tomato, chopped
1 medium green bell pepper, chopped	6 tablespoons reduced-fat Cheddar cheese, shredded
1 envelope dry reduced-sodium taco seasoning	¼ cup green onions or chives, chopped
½ cup water	¼ cup fat-free sour cream or fat-free plain yogurt
4 cups reduced-sodium vegetable juice	Baked tortilla or corn chips
1 cup chunky salsa	

1. Brown meat with onion in nonstick skillet. Drain. 2. Combine all soup ingredients in crock pot. 3. Cover. Cook on low 6 to 8 hours. 4. Serve with your choice of toppings.

Chinese Chicken Soup

Prep time: 5 minutes | Cook time: 1 to 2 hours | Serves 6

3 (14½-ounce / 411-g) cans chicken broth
1 (16-ounce / 454-g) package frozen stir-fry vegetable blend

2 cups cooked chicken, cubed
1 teaspoon minced fresh ginger root
1 teaspoon soy sauce

1. Mix all ingredients in crock pot. 2. Cover and cook on high for 1 to 2 hours, depending upon how crunchy or soft you like your vegetables to be.

Barley-Mushroom Soup

Prep time: 15 minutes | Cook time: 7 to 8 hours | Serves 8

6 cups sliced fresh mushrooms
2 large onions, chopped
3 cloves garlic, minced
1 cup chopped celery
1 cup chopped carrots
5 cups water, divided
¼ cup dry quick-cooking pearl barley
4 cups low-sodium beef broth
4 teaspoons Worcestershire sauce

1 to 1½ teaspoons salt (optional)
1½ teaspoons dried basil
1½ teaspoons dried parsley flakes
1 teaspoon dill weed
1½ teaspoons dried oregano
½ teaspoon salt-free seasoning blend
½ teaspoon dried thyme
½ teaspoon garlic powder

1. Combine all ingredients in crock pot. 2. Cook on low 7 to 8 hours, or until vegetables are done to your liking.

Ground Beef Vegetable Soup

Prep time: 15 minutes | Cook time: 8 to 9 hours | Serves 10

1 pound (454 g) ground beef
1 (46-ounce / 1.3-kg) can tomato, or V-8, juice
1 (16-ounce / 454-g) package frozen mixed vegetables,

thawed
2 cups frozen cubed hash browns, thawed
1 envelope dry onion soup mix

1. Brown beef in nonstick skillet on stovetop. Drain. 2. Place beef in crock pot. Stir in remaining ingredients. 3. Cover and cook on low 8 to 9 hours, or until vegetables are cooked through.

Easy Vegetable Soup

Prep time: 20 minutes | Cook time: 8 to 10 hours | Serves 8 to 10

1 pound (454 g) ground beef, browned
1 cup chopped onions
1 (15-ounce / 425-g) can kidney beans or butter beans, undrained
1 cup sliced carrots
¼ cup rice, uncooked
1 quart stewed tomatoes

3½ cups water
5 beef bouillon cubes
1 tablespoon parsley flakes
1 teaspoon salt
⅛ teaspoon pepper
¼ teaspoon dried basil
1 bay leaf

1. Combine all ingredients in crock pot. 2. Cover. Cook on low 8 to 10 hours.

Wonderful Clam Chowder

Prep time: 15 minutes | Cook time: 6 to 7 hours | Serves 4 to 6

2 (12-ounce / 340-g) cans evaporated milk
1 evaporated milk can of water
2 (6-ounce / 170-g) cans whole clams, undrained
1 (6-ounce / 170-g) can minced

clams, undrained
1 small onion, chopped
2 small potatoes, diced
2 tablespoons cornstarch
¼ cup water

1. Combine all ingredients except cornstarch and ¼ cup water in crock pot. 2. Cover. Cook on low 6 to 7 hours. 3. One hour before end of cooking time, mix cornstarch and ¼ cup water together. When smooth, stir into soup. Stir until soup thickens.

Hearty Lentil and Sausage Stew

Prep time: 10 minutes | Cook time: 4 to 6 hours | Serves 6

2 cups dry lentils, picked over and rinsed
1 (14½-ounce / 411-g) can diced tomatoes
8 cups canned chicken broth or

water
1 tablespoon salt
½ to 1 pound (227 to 454 g) pork or beef sausage, cut into 2-inch pieces

1. Place lentils, tomatoes, chicken broth, and salt in crock pot. Stir to combine. Place sausage pieces on top. 2. Cover and cook on low 4 to 6 hours, or until lentils are tender but not dry or mushy.

Cheese and Corn Chowder

Prep time: 10 minutes | Cook time: 5 to 7 hours | Serves 8

¾ cup water	whole-kernel corn, drained
½ cup chopped onions	1 (15-ounce / 425-g) can cream-
1½ cups sliced carrots	style corn
1½ cups chopped celery	3 cups milk
1 teaspoon salt	1½ cup shredded Cheddar
½ teaspoon pepper	cheese
1 (15¼-ounce / 432-g) can	

1. Combine water, onions, carrots, celery, salt, and pepper in crock pot. 2. Cover. Cook on high 4 to 6 hours. 3. Add corn, milk, and cheese. Heat on high 1 hour, and then turn to low until you are ready to eat.

Many-Veggies Beef Stew

Prep time: 25 minutes | Cook time: 10 to 11 hours | Serves 14 to 18

2 to 3 pounds (907 g to 1.4 kg) beef, cubed	1 large onion, chopped
1 (16-ounce / 454-g) package frozen green beans or mixed vegetables	4 medium potatoes, peeled and chopped
	1 (10¾-ounce / 305-g) can tomato soup
1 (16-ounce / 454-g) package frozen corn	1 (10¾-ounce / 305-g) can celery soup
1 (16-ounce / 454-g) package frozen peas	1 (10¾-ounce / 305-g) can mushroom soup
2 pounds (907 g) carrots, chopped	Bell pepper, chopped (optional)

1. Combine all ingredients in 2 (4-quart) crock pots (this is a very large recipe). 2. Cover. Cook on low 10 to 11 hours.

Creamy Tomato Soup

Prep time: 20 minutes | Cook time: 1½ hours | Serves 6

1 (26-ounce / 737-g) can condensed tomato soup, plus 6 ounces (170 g) water to equal 1 quart	Half a stick butter
	8 tablespoons flour
	1 quart milk (whole or reduced-fat)
½ teaspoon salt (optional)	

1. Put tomato soup, salt if you wish, and butter in crock pot. Blend

well. 2. Cover and cook on high for 1 hour. 3. Meanwhile, place flour and 1 cup milk in 2-quart microwave-safe container. Whisk together until big lumps disappear. Then whisk in remaining milk until only small lumps remain. 4. Place flour-milk mixture in microwave and cook on high for 3 minutes. Remove and stir until smooth. Return to microwave and cook on high for another 3 minutes. 5. Add thickened milk slowly to hot soup in crock pot. 6. Heat thoroughly for 10 to 15 minutes.

Mjeddrah or Esau's Lentil Soup

Prep time: 15 minutes | Cook time: 6 to 8 hours | Serves 8

1 cup chopped carrots	6 cups water
1 cup diced celery	1 pound (454 g) lentils, washed
2 cups chopped onions	and drained
1 tablespoon olive oil or butter	Garden salad
2 cups brown rice	Vinaigrette
1 tablespoon olive oil or butter	

1. Sauté carrots, celery, and onions in 1 tablespoon oil in skillet. When soft and translucent place in crock pot. 2. Brown rice in 1 tablespoon oil until dry. Add to crock pot. 3. Stir in water and lentils. 4. Cover. Cook on high 6 to 8 hours. 5. When thoroughly cooked, serve 1 cup each in individual soup bowls. Cover each with a serving of fresh garden salad (lettuce, spinach leaves, chopped tomatoes, minced onions, chopped bell peppers, sliced olives, sliced radishes). Pour favorite vinaigrette over all.

Karen's Split Pea Soup

Prep time: 15 minutes | Cook time: 7 hours | Serves 6

2 carrots	2 tablespoons olive oil
2 ribs celery	1 bay leaf
1 onion	1 teaspoon dried thyme
1 parsnip	4 cups chicken broth
1 leek (keep 3 inches of green)	4 cups water
1 ripe tomato	1 teaspoon salt
1 ham hock	¼ teaspoon pepper
1¾ cups dried split peas, washed with stones removed	2 teaspoons chopped fresh parsley

1. Cut all vegetables into ¼-inch pieces and place in crock pot. Add remaining ingredients except salt, pepper, and parsley. 2. Cover. Cook on high 7 hours. 3. Remove ham hock. Shred meat from bone and return meat to pot. 4. Season soup with salt and pepper. Stir in parsley. Serve immediately.

Chicken Noodle Soup

Prep time: 10 minutes | Cook time: 4 to 8 hours |
Serves 6 to 8

2 cups chicken, cubed	10 cups water
1 (15¼-ounce / 432-g) can corn, or 2 cups frozen corn	10 to 12 chicken bouillon cubes
1 cup frozen peas or green beans	3 tablespoons bacon drippings
	½ package dry kluski (or other very sturdy) noodles

1. Combine all ingredients except noodles in crock pot. 2. Cover. Cook on high 4 to 6 hours, or on low 6 to 8 hours. Add noodles during last 2 hours. 3. Serve.

Cheeseburger Soup

Prep time: 15 minutes | Cook time: 8 to 9 hours |
Serves 6

1 pound (454 g) ground turkey	1 cup non-fat milk
1 cup chopped onions	2 cups water
½ cup chopped green bell peppers	2 tablespoons flour
2 ribs celery, chopped	8 ounces (227 g) low-fat Cheddar cheese, shredded
1 (20-ounce / 567-g) beef broth	

1. Brown turkey in nonstick skillet. Spoon into crock pot. 2. Add vegetables to crock pot. 3. Heat broth, milk, and water in skillet. Sprinkle flour over liquid. Stir until smooth and let boil for 3 minutes. 4. Pour into crock pot. 5. Cover. Cook on low 6 hours. Then add cheese and cook another 2 to 3 hours.

Overnight Bean Soup

Prep time: 10 minutes | Cook time: 5¼ to 11¼ hours
| Serves 6 to 8

1 pound (454 g) dry small white beans	1 bay leaf
6 cups water	½ teaspoon dried thyme
2 cups boiling water	½ teaspoon salt
2 large carrots, diced	¼ teaspoon pepper
3 ribs celery, diced	¼ cup chopped fresh parsley
2 teaspoons chicken bouillon granules, or 2 chicken bouillon cubes	1 envelope dry onion soup mix
	Crispy, crumbled bacon (optional)

1. Rinse beans. Combine beans and 6 cups water in saucepan. Bring to boil. Reduce heat to low and simmer 2 minutes. Remove from heat. Cover and let stand 1 hour or overnight. 2. Place beans and soaking water in crock pot. 3. Add 2 cups boiling water, carrots, celery, bouillon, bay leaf, thyme, salt, and pepper. Cover. Cook on high 5 to 5½ hours, or on low 10 to 11 hours, until beans are tender. 4. Stir in parsley and soup mix. Cover. Cook on high 10 to 15 minutes. 5. Remove bay leaf. Garnish individual servings with bacon.

Hamburger Vegetable Stew

Prep time: 20 minutes | Cook time: 8 to 10 hours |
Serves 8

2 pounds (907 g) ground beef	1 tablespoon Worcestershire sauce
1 medium onion, chopped	¼ teaspoon dried oregano
1 garlic clove, minced	¼ teaspoon dried basil
2 cups tomato juice	¼ teaspoon dried thyme
2 to 3 carrots, sliced	Dash of hot pepper sauce
2 to 3 ribs celery, sliced	2 tablespoons dry onion soup mix, or 1 beef bouillon cube
Half a green pepper, chopped	
2 cups green beans	1 teaspoon salt
2 medium potatoes, cubed	¼ teaspoon pepper
2 cups water	

1. Brown meat and onion in saucepan. Drain. Stir in garlic and tomato juice. Heat to boiling. 2. Combine all ingredients in crock pot. 3. Cover. Cook on low 8 to 10 hours.

White Bean and Barley Soup

Prep time: 15 minutes | Cook time: 8 to 10 hours |
Serves 12

1 large onion, chopped	peppers, chunked
2 garlic cloves, minced	2 celery ribs, chunked
1 tablespoon olive or canola oil	½ cup quick-cooking barley
2 (24-ounce / 680-g) cans Great Northern beans, undrained	¼ cup chopped fresh parsley
	2 bay leaves
4 cups no-fat, low-sodium chicken broth	½ teaspoon dried thyme
4 cups water	¼ teaspoon black pepper
2 large carrots, chunked	1 (28-ounce / 794-g) can diced tomatoes, undrained
2 medium green or red bell	

1. Sauté onion and garlic in oil in skillet until just wilted. 2. Combine all ingredients in crock pot. 3. Cook on low 8 to 10 hours. 4. Discard bay leaves before serving.

Joyce's Minestrone

Prep time: 15 minutes | Cook time: 4 to 16 hours | Serves 6

3½ cups beef broth
1 (28-ounce / 794-g) can crushed tomatoes
2 medium carrots, thinly sliced
½ cup chopped onion
½ cup chopped celery
2 medium potatoes, thinly sliced
1 to 2 garlic cloves, minced

1 (16-ounce / 454-g) can red kidney beans, drained
2 ounces (57 g) thin spaghetti, broken into 2-inch pieces
2 tablespoons parsley flakes
2 to 3 teaspoons dried basil
1 to 2 teaspoons dried oregano
1 bay leaf

1. Combine all ingredients in crock pot. 2. Cover. Cook on low 10 to 16 hours, or on high 4 to 6 hours. 3. Remove bay leaf. Serve.

Pork-Veggie Stew

Prep time: 15 minutes | Cook time: 6 hours | Serves 8

2 pounds (907 g) boneless pork loin, cut into 1-inch cubes
8 medium potatoes, peeled and cut into 2-inch pieces

6 large carrots, peeled and cut into 2-inch pieces
1 cup ketchup
2¼ cups water, divided

1. Brown pork cubes in a large nonstick skillet. 2. Lightly spray crock pot with nonstick cooking spray. 3. Place all ingredients except ketchup and ¼ cup water in crock pot. 4. Cover and cook on high 5 hours. One hour before serving, combine ketchup with ¼ cup water. Pour over stew. Cook one more hour.

Hamburger-Lentil Soup

Prep time: 20 minutes | Cook time: 4 to 10 hours | Serves 8

1 pound (454 g) ground beef
½ cup chopped onions
4 carrots, diced
3 ribs celery, diced
1 garlic clove, minced, or 1 teaspoon garlic powder
1 quart tomato juice

1 tablespoon salt
2 cups dry lentils, washed with stones removed
1 quart water
½ teaspoon dried marjoram
1 tablespoon brown sugar

1. Brown ground beef and onion in skillet. Drain. 2. Combine all ingredients in crock pot. 3. Cover. Cook on low 8 to 10 hours, or on high 4 to 6 hours.

Southwestern Soup

Prep time: 15 minutes | Cook time: 6 to 8 hours | Serves 4

2 (14-ounce / 397-g) cans beef broth
½ cup sliced carrots
½ cup diced onions
1 cup diced potatoes
1 garlic clove, minced
1 (8-ounce / 227-g) can or 1 cup home-canned crushed tomatoes
1 tablespoon Worcestershire sauce
Salsa to taste
Garnishes:

Shredded cheese
Diced avocados
Diced green peppers
Diced cucumbers
1 (6-ounce / 170-g) can cooked and peeled tiny shrimp
1 cup cooked ham, diced
1 cup sliced green onion
3 hard-cooked eggs, chopped
1 cup diced tomatoes
Sour cream

1. Combine broth, carrots, onions, potatoes, garlic, tomatoes, and Worcestershire sauce in crock pot. Cook on low 6 to 8 hours. 2. Before serving, stir in salsa, sampling as you go to get the right balance of flavors. 3. Serve the soup in bowls. Offer your choice of garnishes as toppings.

Santa Fe Stew

Prep time: 20 minutes | Cook time: 4½ to 6½ hours | Serves 4 to 6

2 pounds (907 g) sirloin or stewing meat, cubed
2 tablespoons oil
1 large onion, diced
2 garlic cloves, minced
1½ cups water
1 tablespoon dried parsley flakes
2 beef bouillon cubes
1 teaspoon ground cumin
½ teaspoon salt
3 carrots, sliced
1 (14½-ounce / 411-g) can

diced tomatoes
1 (14½-ounce / 411-g) can green beans, drained, or 1 pound (454 g) frozen green beans
1 (14½-ounce / 411-g) can corn, drained, or 1 pound (454 g) frozen corn
1 (4-ounce / 113-g) can diced green chilies
3 zucchini squash, diced (optional)

1. Brown meat, onion, and garlic in oil in saucepan until meat is no longer pink. Place in crock pot. 2. Stir in remaining ingredients. 3. Cover. Cook on high 30 minutes. Reduce heat to low and cook 4 to 6 hours.

Chicken Corn Soup

Prep time: 15 minutes | Cook time: 8 to 9 hours | Serves 4 to 6

2 whole boneless, skinless chicken breasts, cubed
1 onion, chopped
1 garlic clove, minced
2 carrots, sliced
2 ribs celery, chopped
2 medium potatoes, cubed
1 teaspoon mixed dried herbs
⅓ cup tomato sauce

1 (12-ounce / 340-g) can cream-style corn
1 (14-ounce / 397-g) whole-kernel corn
3 cups chicken stock
¼ cup chopped Italian parsley
1 teaspoon salt
¼ teaspoon pepper

1. Combine all ingredients except parsley, salt, and pepper in crock pot. 2. Cover. Cook on low 8 to 9 hours, or until chicken is tender. 3. Add parsley and seasonings 30 minutes before serving.

Green Bean and Ham Soup

Prep time: 15 minutes | Cook time: 4¼ to 6¼ hours | Serves 6

1 meaty ham bone, or 2 cups cubed ham
1½ quarts water
1 large onion, chopped
2 to 3 cups cut-up green beans
3 large carrots, sliced
2 large potatoes, peeled and

cubed
1 tablespoon parsley
1 tablespoon summer savory
½ teaspoon salt
¼ teaspoon pepper
1 cup cream or milk

1. Combine all ingredients except cream in crock pot. 2. Cover. Cook on high 4 to 6 hours. 3. Remove ham bone. Cut off meat and return to crock pot. 4. Turn to low. Stir in cream or milk. Heat through and serve.

Barley and Chicken Soup

Prep time: 10 minutes | Cook time: 4 to 6 hours | Serves 5

½ pound (227 g) dry barley
1 small soup chicken, cut up
Fresh celery, as desired

Parsley, as desired
Basil, as desired
Carrots, as desired

1. Combine all ingredients in crock pot. Cover with water. 2. Cover. Cook on low 4 to 6 hours. 3. Remove chicken from bones. Discard skin. Return chicken to soup. Continue cooking until barley is soft.

Chicken Vegetable Soup

Prep time: 10 minutes | Cook time: 6 to 8 hours | Serves 6

1 cup frozen corn
2 ribs celery, chopped
1 (6-ounce / 170-g) can tomato paste
¼ cup dry lentils, rinsed
1 tablespoon sugar

1 tablespoon Worcestershire sauce
2 teaspoons dried parsley flakes
1 teaspoon dried marjoram
2 cups cooked chicken breast, cubed

1. Combine all ingredients in crock pot except chicken. 2. Cover. Cook on low 6 to 8 hours. Stir in chicken 1 hour before the end of the cooking time.

Beef Barley Stew

Prep time: 15 minutes | Cook time: 9 to 10 hours | Serves 6

½ pound (227 g) lean round steak, cut in ½-inch cubes
4 carrots, peeled and cut in ¼-inch slices
1 cup chopped yellow onions
½ cup coarsely chopped green bell peppers
1 clove garlic, pressed
½ pound (227 g) fresh button mushrooms, quartered

¾ cup dry pearl barley
½ teaspoon salt
¼ teaspoon ground black pepper
½ teaspoon dried thyme
½ teaspoon dried sweet basil
1 bay leaf
5 cups fat-free, low-sodium beef broth

1. Combine all ingredients in crock pot. 2. Cover. Cook on low 9 to 10 hours.

Ruth's Split Pea Soup

Prep time: 15 minutes | Cook time: 12 hours | Serves 6 to 8

1 pound (454 g) bulk sausage, browned and drained
6 cups water
1 bag (2¼ cups) dry split peas
2 medium potatoes, diced

1 onion, chopped
½ teaspoon dried marjoram, or thyme
½ teaspoon pepper

1. Wash and sort dried peas, removing any stones. Then combine all ingredients in crock pot. 2. Cover. Cook on low 12 hours.

Chicken Tortilla Soup

Prep time: 10 minutes | Cook time: 8 hours | Serves 6 to 8

4 chicken breast halves
2 (15-ounce / 425-g) cans black beans, undrained
2 (15-ounce / 425-g) cans Mexican stewed tomatoes, or Rotel tomatoes
1 cup salsa, your choice of heat
1 (4-ounce / 113-g) can chopped green chilies
1 (14½-ounce / 411-g) can tomato sauce
Tortilla chips
2 cups shredded cheese

1. Combine all ingredients except chips and cheese in large crock pot. 2. Cover. Cook on low 8 hours. 3. Just before serving, remove chicken breasts and slice into bite-sized pieces. Stir into soup. 4. To serve, put a handful of chips in each individual soup bowl. Ladle soup over chips. Top with cheese.

Lidia's Egg Drop Soup

Prep time: 10 minutes | Cook time: 1 hour | Serves 8

2 (14½-ounce / 411-g) cans fat-free, low-sodium chicken broth
1 quart water
2 tablespoons fish sauce
¼ teaspoon salt
4 tablespoons cornstarch
1 cup cold water
2 eggs, beaten
1 chopped green onion
¼ teaspoon black pepper

1. Combine broth and water in large saucepan. 2. Add fish sauce and salt. Bring to boil. 3. Mix cornstarch into cold water until smooth. Add to soup. Bring to boil while stirring. Remove from heat. 4. Pour beaten eggs into thickened broth, but do not stir. Instead, pull fork through soup with 2 strokes. 5. Transfer to crock pot. Add green onions and pepper. 6. Cover. Cook on low 1 hour. Keep warm in cooker or serve.

Everyone's Hungry Soup

Prep time: 45 minutes | Cook time: 8 to 10 hours | Serves 20 to 25

6 thick slices bacon
3 pounds (1.4 kg) boneless beef stewing meat, cubed
1 pound (454 g) boneless pork, cubed
3 (14½-ounce / 411-g) cans tomatoes
1 (10-ounce / 283-g) can Rotel
tomatoes and chilies
3 celery ribs, chopped
3 large onions, chopped
Garlic to taste
Salt to taste
Pepper to taste
½ cup Worcestershire sauce
2 tablespoons chili powder
2 cups water
6 to 8 medium potatoes, peeled and cubed
1 pound (454 g) carrots, sliced
1 (15-ounce / 425-g) can English peas, undrained
1 (14½-ounce / 411-g) can green beans, undrained
1 (15¼-ounce / 432-g) can corn, undrained
1 pound (454 g) cut-up okra (optional)

1. Fry bacon in skillet until crisp. Remove bacon, but reserve drippings. Crumble bacon and divide between 2 large (6-quart or larger) crock pots. 2. Brown stewing beef and pork in skillet in bacon drippings. 3. Combine all ingredients and divide between crock pots. 4. Cover. Cook on low 8 to 10 hours. 5. Serve.

Cassoulet Chowder

Prep time: 25 minutes | Cook time: 11½ hours | Serves 8 to 10

1¼ cups dry pinto beans
4 cups water
1 (12-ounce / 340-g) package brown-and-serve sausage links, cooked and drained
2 cups cooked chicken, cubed
2 cups cooked ham, cubed
1½ cups sliced carrots
1 (8-ounce / 227-g) can tomato sauce
¾ cup dry red wine
½ cup chopped onions
½ teaspoon garlic powder
1 bay leaf

1. Combine beans and water in large saucepan. Bring to boil. Reduce heat and simmer 1½ hours. Refrigerate beans and liquid 4 to 8 hours. 2. Combine all ingredients in crock pot. 3. Cover. Cook on low 8 to 10 hours, or on 4. High 4 hours. If the chowder seems too thin, remove lid during last 30 minutes of cooking time to allow it to thicken. Remove bay leaf before serving.

Mexican Black Bean Soup

Prep time: 10 minutes | Cook time: 6 to 8 hours | Serves 8

1 (28-ounce / 794-g) can fat-free low-sodium chicken broth
1 cup chopped onions
2 teaspoons minced garlic
3 cups fat-free black beans
2 teaspoons chili powder
¾ teaspoon ground cumin
1 (28-ounce / 794-g) can Mexican tomatoes with green chilies or jalapeños
¾ teaspoon lemon juice
1 bunch green onions
Fat-free sour cream

1.Combine all ingredients except green onions and sour cream in crock pot. 2. Cover. Cook on low 6 to 8 hours. 3. Top each individual serving with sliced green onions sprinkled over a spoonful of sour cream.

Tasty Clam Chowder

Prep time: 15 minutes | Cook time: 2½ hours | Serves 8

2 (1-pound / 454-g) cans low-fat, low-sodium chicken broth

3 large potatoes, peeled and diced finely

2 large onions, chopped finely

1 (1-pound / 454-g) can creamed corn

1 carrot, chopped finely

1 dozen littleneck clams, or 3 (6-ounce / 170-g) cans minced clams

2 cups low-fat milk

¼ teaspoon black pepper

¼ teaspoon salt

2 tablespoons chopped fresh parsley

6 slices bacon, well cooked, drained and crumbled (optional)

1. Pour broth into crock pot. 2. Add potatoes, onions, creamed corn, and carrot. 3. Cover. Cook on high 1 hour. Stir. Cook on high another hour. 4. Using a potato masher, mash potatoes coarsely to thicken soup. 5. Add clams, milk, salt, black pepper, salt, and parsley. 6. Cover. Cook on high 20 minutes. 7. Garnish with crumbled bacon, if desired.

Chapter 10 Pizzas, Wraps, and Sandwiches

Barbecue Sauce and Hamburgers

Prep time: 25 minutes | Cook time: 5 to 6 hours |
Makes 6 sandwiches

1 (14¾-ounce / 418-g) can beef gravy
½ cup ketchup
½ cup chili sauce
1 tablespoon Worcestershire sauce
1 tablespoon prepared mustard
6 grilled hamburger patties
6 slices cheese (optional)

1. Combine all ingredients except hamburger patties and cheese slices in crock pot. 2. Add hamburger patties. 3. Cover. Cook on low 5 to 6 hours. 4. Serve in buns, each topped with a slice of cheese if you like.

Barbecued Ham Sandwiches

Prep time: 7 minutes | Cook time: 5 hours | Makes 4
to 6 sandwiches

1 pound (454 g) chipped turkey ham or chipped honey-glazed ham
1 small onion, finely diced
½ cup ketchup
1 tablespoon vinegar
3 tablespoons brown sugar
Buns, for serving

1. Place half of meat in greased crock pot. 2. Combine other ingredients. Pour half of mixture over meat. Repeat layers. 3. Cover. Cook on low 5 hours. 4. Fill buns and serve.

Sloppy Joes Italia

Prep time: 15 minutes | Cook time: 3 to 4 hours |
Makes 12 sandwiches

1½ pounds (680 g) ground turkey, browned in nonstick skillet
1 cup chopped onions
2 cups low-sodium tomato sauce
1 cup fresh mushrooms, sliced
2 tablespoons Splenda
1 to 2 tablespoons Italian seasoning, according to your taste preference
12 reduced-calorie hamburger buns
12 slices low-fat Mozzarella

cheese (optional)

1. Place ground turkey, onions, tomato sauce, and mushrooms in crock pot. 2. Stir in Splenda and Italian seasoning. 3. Cover. Cook on low 3 to 4 hours. 4. Serve ¼ cup of Sloppy Joe mixture on each bun, topped with cheese, if desired.

Barbecued Beef Sandwiches

Prep time: 10 minutes | Cook time: 10 to 12 hours |
Makes 18 to 20 sandwiches

1 (3½- to 4-pound / 1.6- to 1.8-kg) beef round steak, cubed
1 cup finely chopped onions
½ cup firmly packed brown sugar
1 tablespoon chili powder
½ cup ketchup
⅓ cup cider vinegar
1 (12-ounce / 340-g) can beer
1 (6-ounce / 170-g) can tomato paste
Buns

1. Combine all ingredients except buns in crock pot. 2. Cover. Cook on low 10 to 12 hours. 3. Remove beef from sauce with slotted spoon. 4. Place in large bowl. Shred with 2 forks. Add 2 cups sauce from crock pot to shredded beef. Mix well. 5. Pile into buns and serve immediately.

Beef Pitas

Prep time: 15 minutes | Cook time: 3 to 4 hours |
Makes 2 sandwiches

½ pound (227 g) beef or pork, cut into small cubes
½ teaspoon dried oregano
Dash of black pepper
1 cup chopped fresh tomatoes
2 tablespoons diced fresh green
bell peppers
¼ cup nonfat sour cream
1 teaspoon red wine vinegar
1 teaspoon vegetable oil
2 large pita breads, heated and cut in half

1. Place meat in crock pot. Sprinkle with oregano and black pepper. 2. Cook on low 3 to 4 hours. 3. In a separate bowl, combine tomatoes, green peppers, sour cream, vinegar, and oil. 4. Fill pitas with meat. Top with vegetable and sour cream mixture.

Tangy Barbecue Sandwiches

Prep time: 20 minutes | Cook time: 7 to 9 hours |
Makes 14 to 18 sandwiches

3 cups chopped celery	2 tablespoons brown sugar
1 cup chopped onions	1 teaspoon chili powder
1 cup ketchup	1 teaspoon salt
1 cup barbecue sauce	½ teaspoon pepper
1 cup water	½ teaspoon garlic powder
2 tablespoons vinegar	1 (3- to 4-pound / 1.4- to 1.8-kg)
2 tablespoons Worcestershire	boneless chuck roast
sauce	14 to 18 hamburger buns

1. Combine all ingredients except roast and buns in crock pot. When well mixed, add roast. 2. Cover. Cook on high 6 to 7 hours. 3. Remove roast. Cool and shred meat. Return to sauce. Heat well. 4. Serve on buns.

Zesty French Sandwiches

Prep time: 5 minutes | Cook time: 8 hours | Makes 6 to 8 sandwiches

1 (4-pound / 1.8-kg) beef roast	condensed French onion soup
1 (10½-ounce / 298-g) can beef	1 (12-ounce / 340-g) bottle of
broth	beer
1 (10½-ounce / 298-g) can	6 to 8 French rolls or baguettes

1. Pat roast dry and place in crock pot. 2. In a mixing bowl, combine beef broth, onion soup, and beer. Pour over meat. 3. Cover and cook on low 8 hours, or until meat is tender but not dry. 4. Split rolls or baguettes. Warm in the oven or microwave until heated through. 5. Remove meat from cooker and allow to rest for 10 minutes. Then shred with two forks, or cut on the diagonal into thin slices, and place in rolls. Serve.

Middle-Eastern Sandwiches (for a crowd)

Prep time: 50 minutes | Cook time: 6 to 8 hours |
Makes 10 to 16 sandwiches

4 pounds (1.8 kg) boneless beef	paste
or venison, cut in ½-inch cubes	1 teaspoon dried oregano
4 tablespoons cooking oil	1 teaspoon dried basil
2 cups chopped onions	½ teaspoon dried rosemary
2 garlic cloves, minced	2 teaspoons salt
1 cup dry red wine	Dash of pepper
1 (6-ounce / 170-g) can tomato	¼ cup cold water

¼ cup cornstarch	diced
Pita pocket breads	1 large cucumber, seeded and
2 cups shredded lettuce	diced
1 large tomato, seeded and	8 ounces (227 g) plain yogurt

1. Brown meat, 1 pound (454 g) at a time, in skillet in 1 tablespoon oil. Reserve drippings and transfer meat to crock pot. 2. Sauté onion and garlic in drippings until tender. Add to meat. 3. Add wine, tomato paste, oregano, basil, rosemary, salt, and pepper. 4. Cover. Cook on low 6 to 8 hours. 5. Turn cooker to high. Combine cornstarch and water in small bowl until smooth. Stir into meat mixture. Cook until bubbly and thickened, stirring occasionally. 6. Split pita breads to make pockets. Fill each with meat mixture, lettuce, tomato, cucumber, and yogurt. 7. Serve.

Wash-Day Sandwiches

Prep time: 10 minutes | Cook time: 6 to 7 hours |
Makes 8 to 10 sandwiches

1½ to 2 pounds (680 to 907 g)	quartered
lean lamb or beef, cubed	1 quart water
2 (15-ounce / 425-g) cans	1 teaspoon salt
garbanzo beans, drained	1 tomato, peeled and quartered
2 (15-ounce / 425-g) cans white	1 teaspoon turmeric
beans, drained	3 tablespoons fresh lemon juice
2 medium onions, peeled and	8 to 10 pita bread pockets

1. Combine ingredients in crock pot. 2. Cover. Cook on high 6 to 7 hours. 3. Lift stew from cooker with a strainer spoon and stuff in pita bread pockets.

Beach Boy's Pot Roast

Prep time: 10 minutes | Cook time: 8 to 12 hours |
Makes 6 to 8 sandwiches

1 (3- to 4-pound / 1.4- to 1.8-kg)	undrained
chuck or top round roast	6 to 8 large hoagie rolls
8 to 12 slivers of garlic	12 to 16 slices of your favorite
1 (32-ounce / 907-g) jar	cheese
pepperoncini peppers,	

1. Cut slits into roast with a sharp knife and insert garlic slivers. 2. Place beef in crock pot. Spoon peppers and all of their juice over top. 3. Cover and cook on low 8 to 12 hours, or until meat is tender but not dry. 4. Remove meat from cooker and allow to cool. Then use 2 forks to shred the beef. 5. Spread on hoagie rolls and top with cheese.

Appendix Measurement Conversion Chart

MEASUREMENT CONVERSION CHART

VOLUME EQUIVALENTS(DRY)

US STANDARD	METRIC (APPROXIMATE)
1/8 teaspoon	0.5 mL
1/4 teaspoon	1 mL
1/2 teaspoon	2 mL
3/4 teaspoon	4 mL
1 teaspoon	5 mL
1 tablespoon	15 mL
1/4 cup	59 mL
1/2 cup	118 mL
3/4 cup	177 mL
1 cup	235 mL
2 cups	475 mL
3 cups	700 mL
4 cups	1 L

WEIGHT EQUIVALENTS

US STANDARD	METRIC (APPROXIMATE)
1 ounce	28 g
2 ounces	57 g
5 ounces	142 g
10 ounces	284 g
15 ounces	425 g
16 ounces (1 pound)	455 g
1.5 pounds	680 g
2 pounds	907 g

VOLUME EQUIVALENTS(LIQUID)

US STANDARD	US STANDARD (OUNCES)	METRIC (APPROXIMATE)
2 tablespoons	1 fl.oz.	30 mL
1/4 cup	2 fl.oz.	60 mL
1/2 cup	4 fl.oz.	120 mL
1 cup	8 fl.oz.	240 mL
1 1/2 cup	12 fl.oz.	355 mL
2 cups or 1 pint	16 fl.oz.	475 mL
4 cups or 1 quart	32 fl.oz.	1 L
1 gallon	128 fl.oz.	4 L

TEMPERATURES EQUIVALENTS

FAHRENHEIT(F)	CELSIUS(C) (APPROXIMATE)
225 °F	107 °C
250 °F	120 °C
275 °F	135 °C
300 °F	150 °C
325 °F	160 °C
350 °F	180 °C
375 °F	190 °C
400 °F	205 °C
425 °F	220 °C
450 °F	235 °C
475 °F	245 °C
500 °F	260 °C